2-06

AL CAPONE

Other books in the Heroes and Villains series include:

Heroes and Villains

AL CAPONE

Diane Yancey

**LUCENT
BOOKS** ®

THOMSON
───────✦───────™
GALE

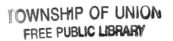
San Diego • Detroit • New York • San Francisco • Cleveland • New Haven, Conn. • Waterville, Maine • London • Munich

THOMSON

———✶———

GALE

© 2003 by Lucent Books. Lucent Books is an imprint of The Gale Group, Inc.,
a division of Thomson Learning, Inc.

Lucent Books® and Thomson Learning™ are trademarks used herein under license.

For more information, contact
Lucent Books
27500 Drake Rd.
Farmington Hills, MI 48331-3535
Or you can visit our Internet site at http://www.gale.com

LIBRARY OF CONGRESS CATALOGING-IN-PUBLICATION DATA

Yancey, Diane.
   Al Capone / by Diane Yancey.
         p. cm. — (Heroes and villains series)
Includes bibliographical references and index.
Summary: Discusses the early life of Al Capone, lawlessness, prohibition,
gangsters, family life, prison, and legacy of Al Capone.
   ISBN 1-56006-949-X (hardback : alk. paper)
   1. Capone, Al, 1899–1947—Juvenile literature. 2. Criminals—Illinois—Chicago—
Biography—Juvenile literature. 3. Organized crime—Illinois—Chicago—History—
Juvenile literature. I. Title. II. Series. III. Series: Heroes and villains series
   HV6248 .C17 T36 2003
   364.1'092—dc21
 	
2002003285

Printed in the United States of America

Contents

Foreword

Good and evil are an ever-present feature of human history. Their presence is reflected through the ages in tales of great heroism and extraordinary villainy. Such tales provide insight into human nature, whether they involve two people or two thousand, for the essence of heroism and villainy is found in deeds rather than in numbers. It is the deeds that pique our interest and lead us to wonder what prompts a man or woman to perform such acts.

Samuel Johnson, the eminent eighteenth-century English writer, once wrote, "The two great movers of the human mind are the desire for good, and fear of evil." The pairing of desire and fear, possibly two of the strongest human emotions, helps explain the intense fascination people have with all things good and evil—and by extension, heroic and villainous.

People are attracted to the person who reaches into a raging river to pull a child from what could have been a watery grave for both, and to the person who risks his or her own life to shepherd hundreds of desperate black slaves to safety on the Underground Railroad. We wonder what qualities these heroes possess that enable them to act against self-interest, and even their own survival. We also wonder if, under similar circumstances, we would behave as they do.

Evil, on the other hand, horrifies as well as intrigues us. Few people can look upon the drifter who mutilates and kills a neighbor or the dictator who presides over the torture and murder of thousands of his own citizens without feeling a sense of revulsion. And yet, as Joseph Conrad writes, we experience "the fascination of the abomination." How else to explain the overwhelming success of a book such as Truman Capote's *In Cold Blood*, which examines in horrifying detail a vicious and senseless murder that took place in the American heartland in the 1960s? The popularity of murder mysteries and Court TV are also evidence of the human fascination with villainy.

Most people recoil in the face of such evil. Yet most feel a deep-seated curiosity about the kind of person who could commit a terrible act. It is perhaps a reflection of our innermost fears that we wonder whether we could resist or stand up to such behavior in our presence or even if we ourselves possess the capacity to commit such terrible crimes.

The Lucent Books Heroes and Villains series capitalizes on our fascination with the perpetrators of both good and evil by introducing readers to some of history's most revered heroes and hated villains. These include heroes such as Frederick Douglass, who knew firsthand the humiliation of slavery and, at great risk to himself, publicly fought to abolish the institution of slavery in America. It also includes villains such as Adolf Hitler, who is remembered both for the devastation of Europe and for the murder of 6 million Jews and thousands of Gypsies, Slavs, and others whom Hitler deemed unworthy of life.

Each book in the Heroes and Villains series examines the life story of a hero or villain from history. Generous use of primary and secondary source quotations gives readers eyewitness views of the life and times of each individual as well as enlivens the narrative. Notes and annotated bibliographies provide stepping-stones to further research.

THE LAWLESS ERA

Al Capone, the most infamous gangster of the 1920s, was born into an America that distrusted and discriminated against anyone who was not white, Anglo-Saxon, and Protestant. This included Jews, Roman Catholics, Blacks, Asians, Hispanics, and emigrants from southern Europe. Italian Americans like the Capones fell into the latter category. They were stereotyped as lazy, stupid, and criminal, unable to learn in school, and unable to blend into American society. "The Italian comes in at the bottom . . . and stays there,"[1] wrote one journalist of the time.

In the slums of New York City where Capone grew up, prejudice against Italians was expressed verbally by the racist slur "dago." He undoubtedly heard it often from young Irish,

America's notorious gangster, Al Capone.

The Booze Trade

Although many Americans believed that the Eighteenth Amendment—Prohibition—would make America a better country, the law triggered widespread lawbreaking and provided a new source of income for outlaws like John Torrio and Al Capone. Author Rich Hornung gives further details in his book Al Capone.

Prohibition tripled the revenues of the most successful racketeers within the first few years. Little John Torrio's organization of brothels and gaming dens netted less than $2 million annually before the ban on alcohol. By the end of 1921, law enforcement officials estimated his organization to gross more than $5 million. Across the country outlaws learned that bribing the police and delivering whiskey were far more profitable than stickups, bank robberies, or jewel heists. Though a variety of gangs would shoot their way into competition for the lucrative booze trade, Prohibition was the first chance for criminals to cast themselves as men of commerce....

As Al Capone would frequently remind the residents of Chicago, "All I ever did was to sell beer and whiskey to our best people.... All I ever did was supply a demand that was pretty popular. Why, the very guys that make my trade good are the boys who yell the loudest at me."

Agents inspect ten-thousand-gallon vats at an illegal distillery found in Detroit.

A police official seizes an illegal still used to manufacture bootleg liquor.

Undoubtedly anti-Italian hostility played a large role in shaping Capone's attitudes toward his family, his country, and the law. He was fiercely proud to be an American, but he felt resentment toward those who despised his people and his roots. One historian points out, "His Italian heritage formed and informed every aspect of his life and career. He belonged both to the Old World . . . and to the New."[2]

"Murder Galore and Crime Unpunished"

By the time Capone turned twenty-one, America was entering the Roaring Twenties, a decade of excess and lawlessness that offered enormous profits for criminals. Prohibition, which took effect in January 1920 and remained the law until 1933, banned the manufacture, sale, and transportation of alcohol in the United States. Professional lawbreakers saw it as their opportunity to make money, and expanded their illegal activities accordingly. They bought breweries, smuggled in liquor from Canada and the Caribbean islands, and financed bootleg, or illegal, operations where cheap liquor was manufactured and sold at high prices. Rival gangs jockeyed for power and tried to eliminate each other, and crime waves swept through cities. In 1926, the *Literary Digest* summed up the situation in Chicago, where Capone had moved in 1920, as "murder galore and crime unpunished."[3]

Sicilian, and Jewish boys who taunted him and his friends as they played on the streets of Brooklyn.

Anti-Italian prejudice was expressed in more destructive ways as well. Because of their heritage, families like the Capones were condemned to live in crowded, disease-ridden neighborhoods, and were unable to make a decent wage. Italian men commonly found work only at the most menial of jobs—working on loading docks, hawking trinkets from street stands, or running small fruit and vegetable stores—and were paid 20 to 40 percent less than other men doing the same kind of work.

Prohibition was only one element that allowed up-and-coming criminals like Capone to become multimillionaires. Dishonest politicians and law enforcement officials in cities like Chicago, New York, and Detroit were willing to take bribes in return for allowing crime to flourish almost uninterrupted. William "Big Bill" Thompson, the mayor of Chicago for most of the 1920s, was one of the most corrupt. "Sure we have crime here," he admitted, "We always will have crime. Chicago is just like any other big city. You can get a man's arm broken for so much, a leg for so much, or beaten up for so much."[4]

Even many ordinary Americans were tolerant of lawbreaking in the 1920s. In fact, they ignored Prohibition, flocked to illegal drinking establishments called speakeasies and nightclubs, danced and drank too much, and drove their cars too fast. Anything that was daring and rebellious was attractive. "Modesty, reticence [restraint], and chivalry was going out of style. . . . Everybody wanted to be modern,—and sophisticated, and smart, to smash the conventions,"[5] observes one historian.

Victim or Villain
The era was custom-made for a clever, ambitious young man like Al Capone.

Celebrity

Al Capone was not the first lawbreaker to capture public interest, but he was one of the most accessible. And those who met him face-to-face—even the most reluctant—were usually impressed. Biographer Robert J. Schoenberg tries to explain their reactions in his book Mr. Capone: The Real—And Complete—Story of Al Capone.

Our decades did not invent 'celebrity.' Society found the same frisson [thrill] in consorting with Capone that one might in having a tame and amiable tiger as a house pet. Here was a certifiably dangerous man, whose very bulk radiated power, a constant lawbreaker who had unarguably killed personally, whose fiat [command] had certainly slaughtered at least dozens, maybe hundreds, slaughter that *continued*. Yet the respectable could consort with him in safety, even with unfeigned [genuine] pleasure. Capone dressed, spoke and acted well, if somewhat floridly [extravagantly]. One contemporary called him 'a fervent handshaker, with an agreeable, well-nigh ingratiating smile.' He flashed it often and easily.

Through a combination of good timing, ruthlessness, and first-rate business skills, he made his way up the ladder of crime until he was one of the most wealthy and powerful men in the United States. A vicious thug who hid his brutality behind a cheerful grin and a warm handshake, he horrified and fascinated the country at the same time. "I can't feel he was all evil, like he's been painted since then," said one Chicagoan. "Sure he was a cold-blooded killer, but he had his good side. I see him as a victim of his time and circumstances."[6]

Victim or villain, Al Capone was the personification of a decade long remembered for its exuberant rowdiness and excess. He represented all that was wrong with America, and some that was good as well. His story is one of a complex and contradictory man who believed in himself, overcame the odds, and became in a peculiar way the epitome of the rags-to-riches character with whom America has always been enthralled.

Chapter One

HEFTY HOOLIGAN

Alphonse (Al) Capone was born on January 17, 1899, in Brooklyn, New York. He was the fourth son of Gabriele and Teresina (Teresa) Capone, an Italian couple who made the transatlantic crossing from Naples, Italy, to America in 1893.

Although most Italians eked out a living through backbreaking labor, Gabriele, a barber by trade, was spared such hardship. Shortly after his arrival in New York, he opened a small barbershop that brought in a modest living. Nevertheless, his income was low, and in the early days he could afford to house his family only in an unfurnished apartment near the Brooklyn Naval Yard.

The neighborhood was rough, marked by saloons, dance halls, tattoo parlors, and drunken sailors. In the Capone apartment, heat came from two stoves, one in the kitchen and another in the parlor. A pipe in the hallway supplied cold water, and a small shack in the backyard served as a communal toilet.

Gabriele and Teresa were an honest, hardworking couple, however, who tried to raise well-behaved, law-abiding children. Despite long hours at work, Gabriele found time to study and become an American citizen in 1906. Teresa stayed home to take care of the boys, all of whom soon had Americanized names. Vincenzo became James; Raffaele, Ralph; Salvatore, Frank; and Alphonse, Al. The Capone home gave no sign that six of the boys who grew up there would be involved in crime, and that the most notorious gangster of the 1920s would rise to power from within its walls.

Little Alphonse

Little Alphonse was a healthy, chubby baby who grew to be a sturdy, street-wise little boy. He was not the youngest in his family for long. Erminio (John or Mimi) was born in 1901; Umberto (Albert) in 1906; Amedoe (Matthew) in 1908; Rose in 1910; and Mafalda in 1912. The boys were full of energy and mischief, but were taught to be respectful of their parents. Rose died shortly after birth, and little Mafalda, named after an Italian princess, was the spoiled darling of the family.

As time passed, the Capones moved from their tiny apartment to a larger one on pleasant, residential Garfield Place, ten minutes away. There, Al started school at the age of five, and, like most children of immigrant parents, was exposed to many American traditions and practices for the first time. He learned American history and the Pledge of Allegiance, heard English spoken constantly, and played with children of different backgrounds.

New York's education system, however, offered little help to immigrant

In this 1890 picture Italian immigrants make neckties in a New York tenement.

An Unremarkable Family

Historians and other experts have been unsuccessful in uncovering any dysfunction in the Capone family that may have caused its young men to become criminals. Historian Laurence Bergreen explains in his book Capone: The Man and His Era.

[The neighbors] recalled the Capones as a quiet, conventional family. The mother, Donna [lady] Teresina as she was known, kept to herself. Her husband, Don [gentleman] Gabriele, made more of an impression, since he was, in the words of one family friend, 'tall and handsome—very good looking.' Like his wife, he was subdued, even when it came to discipline. 'He never hit the kids. He used to talk to them. He used to preach to them, and they listened to their father....'

Nothing about the Capone family was inherently disturbed, violent, or dishonest. The children and the parents were close, there was no apparent mental disability, no traumatic event that sent the boys hurtling into a life of crime. They did not display sociopathic or psychotic personalities; they were not crazy. Nor did they inherit a predilection for a criminal career or belong to a criminal society.... They were a law-abiding, unremarkable Italian-American family with conventional patterns of behavior and frustrations; they displayed no special genius for crime, or anything else, for that matter.

children who needed assistance with schoolwork or unfamiliar routines. Classes were dry and unimaginative. Teachers demanded obedience and used physical force to keep order. Al did not respond well to such treatment. His first grade teacher remembered him as being "swarthy [and] sullen,"[7] a child who was rebellious and inclined to fight.

Al was a relatively good student in the early grades, but as he got older he preferred to skip school. The docks were fascinating to him, and he loved to watch the changing of the U.S. Marine guards inside the navy yard. He also liked to taunt the guards through the fence, and once, when he was ten, one of them got angry. Al dared the older man to fight, and escaped a pounding only because the guard's superior, a corporal, got involved. The episode ended without violence, but the corporal noted Al's fearlessness. He said,

If this kid had a good Marine officer to get hold of him and steer him right, he'd make a good man. But if nothing like this will happen, the kid may drift for a few years until some wise guy picks him up and steers him around and then he'll be heard from one day.[8]

These words were prophetic; Al soon met the "wise guy" the corporal had worried about. On his way to school every day, the boy walked past a building bearing the words "The John Torrio Association." Torrio, known as "Little John" on the streets of Brooklyn, was polite, friendly, and generous to the boys, but rumor had it that he made his living from gambling, prostitution, and racketeering (controlling businesses through threats and violence). Although he left New York for Chicago in 1909, Torrio did not forget young Al who had often run errands for him. Later Torrio would become Capone's mentor in crime. "I looked on Johnny like my adviser and father," Capone later remembered. "[He was] the party who made it possible for me to get my start."[9]

Dropout

By the time he was fourteen, Al was doing so poorly in school that his teacher held him back a grade. The failure was upsetting. He was embarrassed by having to sit with children who were younger and smaller than he. Then, when the same teacher taunted him on his size and lectured him on his poor performance, he swore at her. She hit him. He hit her back.

The attack earned him a trip to the principal's office and a whipping. Al submitted, but vowed never to return to school. His parents were not surprised or dismayed when he broke the news. In their neighborhood, children often dropped out as soon as they were old enough to work, and the Capone boys were not exceptions. Their eldest son, James, had run away from home when he was sixteen. Ralph had quit school when he reached sixth grade. Their only requirement was that Al get a job to help support the family.

Mobster Frankie Yale helped initiate Capone into the criminal world.

The Five Pointers

For Capone and many other young men growing up in New York City, gangs were a way of life, a means of belonging and protecting oneself and one's territory from enemies. A history of some of the most notorious New York gangs is included in the following article entitled "Five Points Gang," found on the Internet at historychannel.com.

In the 1800s, the Irish potato famine drove millions of immigrants to America, where they settled in the worst part of New York City, the Five Points. Known as the center of vice and debauchery [wickedness] throughout the nineteenth century, Five Points was the neighborhood named for the points created by the intersection of Park, Worth, and Baxter streets. With no money and few prospects, many Irishmen turned to a life of crime. The first gangs had colorful nicknames like "The Forty Thieves," "The Dead Rabbit Gang," and the "Plug Uglies." Corrupt politicians quickly learned that they could control blocks of voters—and elections—by buying gang support....

Irish gangs fought the anti-immigrant hoods "The Bowery Boys" for control of the streets, resulting in several deadly riots, the most notable being the "Dead Rabbit Riot" of 1857, a street battle that left over a hundred dead. Five years later, the gangs of the Five Points became involved in the Draft Riots of 1863.... Over a hundred buildings were destroyed and many more were looted. Casualties were estimated at 2,000 dead, more than the [Civil War's] Battle of Bull Run....

The new influx of Italian families in the early 1900s bred what became the most dominant group in American crime. Paul Kelly, a.k.a. Paolo Antonio Vacarelli, formed a mixed ethnic gang called "The Five Pointers." From this gang, and its farm team, "The Five Points Juniors," came some of the most infamous names in American crime—Al Capone, Lucky Luciano, Meyer Lansky, and Bugsy Siegel.

Al had no problem with that. He spent the next few years working at various odd jobs. He was a clerk in a candy store, a pin boy in a bowling alley, and a cutter in a bookbindery. The work did not particularly interest him, though. Life on the streets was more exciting, so he became a member of the South Brooklyn Rippers, a youth gang who took members as young as eleven. He also joined the Five Points Juniors, the juvenile branch of an adult gang notorious for committing violent crimes. Although there is no documentation of Capone's participation in specific gang war incidents, undoubtedly he fought fiercely for the honor of his group when the occasion arose.

As he entered his midteens, Al was invited to join the Five Points gang itself. His sponsor was Frankie Yale, a neighborhood racketeer. Yale also owned the Harvard Inn, a seedy nightclub on Coney Island patronized by prostitutes and hard drinkers. In 1917, he was looking for a muscular youth who could act as bartender, waiter, errand boy, and bouncer. He offered Al Capone the job.

Capone was happy to accept. He proved to be good at the work, too. He had charm, an outgoing personality, and the size and strength to control unruly customers. Historian Laurence Bergreen notes, "The customers . . . liked Al, the jolly way he served up the foamy beer at the bar and occasionally took a turn on the dance floor himself. It was not exalted work, but the job kept him busy and on display."[10]

"A Punch Was Not Enough"

Combined with his authoritative position, Al Capone's stocky body, blunt features, and thinning hair gave people the impression that he was older and more mature than he really was. Many assumed that because he was responsible for keeping order in the bar, he had adult self-control as well.

Capone was still a teen, however, prone to recklessness and bad judgment. He was often ruled by his emotions, especially when a pretty girl was

involved. This became apparent one night in 1917. While he was working at the Harvard Inn, he noticed a shapely young woman, a newcomer to the inn, sitting at one of the tables. Her name was Lena Galluccio, sister of small-time hood Frank Galluccio, who was seated beside her.

Attracted to Lena, Capone chose a straightforward approach. He tried to start a conversation with her, but she was not interested and ignored him. He persisted, and she appealed to her brother, asking him to discourage Capone. Before Frank Galluccio could intervene, however, Capone leaned close to Lena's ear and whispered loud enough for others to hear, "Honey, you have a nice ass, and I mean that as a compliment."[11]

Furious that a stranger should be so disrespectful to his sister, Galluccio sprang to his feet and punched Capone in the stomach. However, as he later recalled, "A punch was not enough to stop Capone."[12] Capone lunged forward, ready to fight Galluccio, but Galluccio pulled out a knife. Before anyone could stop him, he slashed at the bouncer's face. Capone didn't back down. The knife caught him on the left side, cutting a slit from his ear to below the corner of his mouth. Galluccio swiped again, opening a gash on Capone's left jaw and another on his neck under his left ear. Then, Galluccio grabbed his sister and ran.

Onlookers rushed Capone to the hospital, where doctors placed about thirty stitches in his face and told him how lucky he was to be alive. The cut on his neck had come close to his carotid artery, one of the body's primary blood vessels. If it had been severed, he could have bled to death.

When he was released from the hospital, Capone let his friends and associates know that he was looking for revenge. Galluccio was so fearful for his life that he appealed for help to Joseph "Joe the Boss" Masseria. Masseria, who came to the United States from Sicily about 1903, was a major crime lord on the Lower East Side of Manhattan. He listened, then ordered Galluccio and Capone to sit down and talk out their differences. As a result of the meeting, Capone apologized for insulting Lena, and Galluccio apologized for his attack.

The incident passed. Capone's wounds healed, although he was left with ugly scars that embarrassed him throughout his life. He continued on civil terms with Galluccio, but got subtle revenge years later, when, as a millionaire, he hired him to be one of his bodyguards for one hundred dollars a week. He also learned a lesson about the impressive influence a crime lord like Masseria could have. One historian notes, "He had seen the power of the racketeers to intervene in daily affairs and to enforce peace, and he began to learn the potency of restraint."[13]

Young and in Love

By the time he was nineteen, Al Capone had gone out with many pretty girls, both at the Harvard Inn and in neighborhood brothels, houses of prostitution. During one of his

The large scars Capone received from a knife fight in his youth earned him the famous nickname "Scarface."

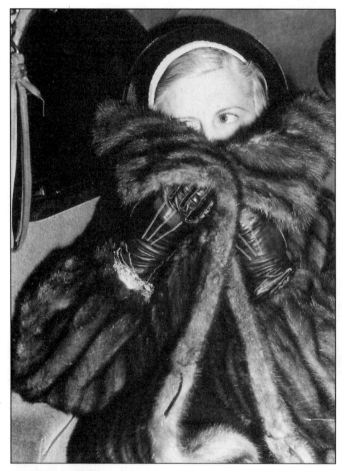

Capone's wife, Mae, shunned publicity and often hid her face from photographers.

would have long-term repercussions later in his life.

Unconcerned about his health or his sexual past, when Al met Mary Coughlin, daughter of Irish construction worker Michael Coughlin, he knew he had found the woman he wanted to marry. Mary, known as Mae, was beautiful, slim, and blond, and came from a respectable middle-class family. Capone found her attractive, and she returned his feelings.

Within a few months, Mae became pregnant. However, in a time when pregnancy before marriage was shameful, the couple waited until three weeks after their baby's birth to get married. The wedding took place on December 30, 1918, at the Coughlin family church. Eight days before, their son Albert Francis Capone, nicknamed "Sonny," had been baptized there.

many contacts with prostitutes he caught syphilis, a sexually transmitted disease for which there was no cure. Because symptoms of syphilis are almost unnoticeable and quickly disappear, he may not have even known that he was infected. If he did note and recognize the infection, he believed he had recovered from it when the symptoms disappeared. He never guessed it

Rough Stuff

Marriage and fatherhood gave Capone the appearance of respectability, but it did not tame his hot temper or eradicate his vicious streak. Instead he remained a callous thug who was soon deeply involved in the criminal world. One day, while on an errand to collect a bet for

Yale, he was hassled by a member of a rival gang. Capone beat the man unconscious, sending him to the hospital, where he remained for weeks. In another instance, Capone encountered resistance from one of Yale's associates, a petty criminal who owed the racketeer fifteen hundred dollars. When the man refused to pay, Capone drew his gun, and fired. It was his first killing, but he took it lightly. He neither appeared shaken, nor tried to excuse his action. Rather, his words revealed a cold-blooded attitude that would later make him notorious. "He deserved what he got,"[14] he reportedly told Yale.

Yale was impressed by Capone's tough determination and willingness to kill, but he also knew that murders brought the threat of reprisal from the police or rival gangs. Yale decided it would be better for Capone to leave New York until interest in the case died down. Thus, Capone, Mae, and Sonny moved to Baltimore, Maryland, in 1919, where Capone worked as a bookkeeper for the Aiello Construction firm. Although he was not used to legitimate employment, he proved to be a satisfactory worker. "Evidently he was a good employee, and evidently my father liked him,"[15] recalls Mike Aiello, son of the company's founder. Capone never revealed whether he enjoyed this period of his life. Undoubtedly it was tame compared with his work at the Harvard Inn.

Frankie Yale

One of Al Capone's earliest employers was Frankie Yale, a young Italian immigrant who found his niche in racketeering at an early age. Like Capone, Yale was a brutal man with a generous streak, as Robert Schoenberg points out in Mr. Capone: The Real—And Complete—Story of Al Capone.

Yale enforced discipline with unending obscenities, unrelenting and indiscriminate brutality. When displeased with his brother Angelo, ten years his junior, Yale beat his brother into a hospital case. Concurrently—and this trait Capone would not have to unlearn—Yale played the gracious don [gentleman], a river of small benefactions to all who honored and respected him. Thieves robbed a poor delicatessen dealer; he found the cash on his counter next morning, replaced by Yale. A fish peddler lost his pushcart; Yale pressed $200 on him saying, "Get a horse, you're too old to walk." When two free-lance hoods tried to shake down Frank Crespi, popular and colorful hat check operator at a neighboring restaurant, Yale personally beat the interlopers senseless.

The Capones' stay in Baltimore ended, however, on November 14, 1920, when Gabriele Capone collapsed and died of a heart attack. Teresa Capone was left without a means of support and with three children still to raise. She appealed to her older sons for help.

Turning Point

None of the Capone boys could contribute enough money to support their extended family comfortably. Al Capone had kept in touch with Johnny Torrio in Chicago, though, and Torrio had heard good things about Capone from mutual friends. In 1920, the gangster offered Capone a place in his growing crime organization, a network of bribery, extortion, violence, and intimidation. The offer appealed to Capone's desire for money and excitement, and he readily agreed. He sent Mae and Sonny back to Brooklyn, and headed west. "He said that he was cut out to do bigger and better things,"[16] Mike Aiello explained after Capone left Baltimore.

The move marked a turning point in Capone's life. Putting a legitimate career aside, he gambled that crime could be extremely profitable if the right man—someone smart, shrewd, and well organized—were in charge of operations. He thought John Torrio was the right man. In retrospect, his judgment was correct. "As an organizer and administrator of underworld affairs John Torrio is unsurpassed in the annals of American crime," one observer later wrote. "He was probably the nearest thing to a real master mind that this country has yet produced."[17] Under Torrio's guidance, Al Capone would rise from petty hoodlum to Chicago crime boss in just five short years.

Chapter Two

TURF WARS

From an early age, Al Capone realized that John Torrio was not a typical criminal. Unlike many gangsters who were burly, hard-living ruffians, Torrio was a pale, mild-mannered man who did not drink, smoke, or carry a gun. He spent most evenings at home with his wife, Ann, whom he shielded from his business dealings. She called him "the best and dearest of husbands" and described their marriage as "one long, unclouded honeymoon."[18]

Torrio was out of the ordinary when it came to his work as well. Although he expected the men who worked for him to use intimidation and violence if a situation warranted it, whenever possible he used negotiation and compromise to get what he wanted. One observer said, "[John Torrio was] the thinking man's criminal,"[19]

and Capone did his best to learn everything he could from him.

Crime Capital

When Torrio moved to Chicago in 1909, he realized that he had found a town where he could break the law without fear of punishment. The city was a sprawling, rowdy metropolis of 3 million people where political corruption was a tradition. Dishonest officials like mayor "Big Bill" Thompson and councilmen John J. Coughlin and Michael "Hinky Dink" Kenna made their fortunes from illegal business dealings. Police, prosecutors, and judges took bribes, tolerated crime, pardoned lawbreakers, and oversaw crooked elections. In the words of one politician of the time, even honest men "had to make compromises with evil, in their judgment, in order to [curb crime and pass legislation that benefited honest Chicago citizens]."[20]

In this setting, Torrio became second in command to "Big Jim" Colosimo, who headed an organized group of criminals. Colosimo, whom Torrio claimed was his uncle, was the owner of the Colosimo Café, a fashionable Chicago restaurant that boasted a world-class chef and first-class entertainment. He appeared hand-

Chicago's North Michigan Avenue in 1925. Capone moved to Chicago to participate in organized crime.

some and courteous as he walked among his clientele, but Colosimo was nevertheless one of the most powerful criminals in Chicago, making his fortune operating bars, brothels, and gambling dens.

Despite his power, Colosimo was always in danger from other criminal gangs who wanted to dominate organized crime in Chicago. Among these were the Genna brothers, the William "Klondike" O'Donnell gang, the Edward "Spike" O'Donnell gang, the Saltis gang, and the Sheldon gang. One of the most noteworthy gangs, known as the Northsiders, was headed by Dion (Deany) O'Banion, who controlled most of the North Side of the city.

Move to Power

When Prohibition became law in 1920, Torrio urged Colosimo to let him expand their crime business to include Chicago breweries, distillers, and truckers that produced and transported liquor. Colosimo reluctantly agreed, but he was not overly interested in business expansion. He had recently fallen in love with a singer named Dale Winter whom he had met in one of his clubs. His mind was always on her.

The situation was frustrating for Torrio who recognized that millions of dollars could be made from illegal liquor, but frequently had to wait for his love-struck boss to approve decisions regarding purchases, expansion, and so

forth. His ambitions were not thwarted for long, however. On May 11, 1920, an unknown killer murdered Colosimo in the foyer of his café. Most people, including the police, believed that Torrio had orchestrated the killing.

When questioned, though, Torrio had an alibi. He also proclaimed his loyalty to Colosimo. "Jim and me were like brothers,"[21] he protested. Nevertheless Torrio benefited from the murder. In the wake of Colosimo's death, he assumed control of a multimillion-dollar-a-year crime business. That business came to be known as "the organization."

Capone Moves Up

When Al Capone arrived in Chicago in early 1920 to work for Torrio and Colosimo, the young man started by managing a brothel, the Four Deuces. In the evening he often stood outside trying to lure in customers. "I saw him there a dozen times," remembered one journalist, "coat collar turned up on winter nights, hands deep in his pockets as he fell in step with a passer-by and mumbled, 'Got some nice-looking girls inside.'"[22] Torrio also used him as a bodyguard, chauffeur, and bartender.

Despite his entry level positions, Capone looked to the future. Aware that the police might one day question his business dealings, he took pains to establish an honest public image. He stocked a vacant storefront next door to the brothel with old furniture and printed up business cards that read "Alphonse Capone, second hand furniture dealer." To carry out illegitimate activities with greater secrecy, he masked his true identity by using various aliases. His favorite was the ordinary, unremarkable "Al Brown."

Capone also made sure that Torrio saw him as a loyal, dependable employee, one who would be worthy of promotion should the opportunity arise. According to one story, Torrio once tested Capone by calling him into his office when a stack of money was lying on his desk. He then left Capone alone with the cash. Torrio returned to find the money untouched. Capone had been smart enough to know that petty pilfering would only bring a quick end to a promising career.

The Man with No Vices

Although he built a multimillion-dollar crime empire, gangster John Torrio seemed unsuited to a life of crime. As John Kobler describes in Capone: The Life and World of Al Capone, *the gangster's daily routine seemed as conventional as that of the most legitimate businessman.*

The contrast between Torrio's professional and private life amazed the few associates familiar with both. Catering to the vices of others, he himself had none. . . . He never smoked, drank or gambled. He ate sparingly. He eschewed [shunned] profane and obscene language and disliked hearing it. He took no interest in any woman but his wife, Ann. With his small, dark, watchful eyes and thin, compressed lips, he seemed perpetually to be deploring the sinful ways of man.

In his daily routine he observed a clocklike regularity. Early every morning, attired in a suit of sober hue and cut, wearing no jewelry save his wedding ring, he would tenderly embrace his wife and either walk the three blocks from their flat . . . to his office on South Wabash [Street] or drive to Burnham [a Chicago suburb]. Then, for the next nine or ten hours he would attend to the minutiae [details] of the brothel business, routing the whores from house to house in order to ensure the regular customers a continual change of faces, cutting corners on the whorehouse food, drink, and linens, calculating the previous night's profits. . . .

Barring some crisis, Torrio would return home at six and, except for an occasional play or concert, not leave it again until morning. His wife would bring him slippers and smoking jacket. After supper they would play pinochle or listen to the phonograph.

James Colosimo was the most powerful man in Chicago's underworld until his death in 1920.

handshake"—in other words, how to use persuasion rather than violence to achieve criminal goals. "We don't want any trouble,"[23] Torrio insisted. Capone tried to remember this, although his temper was hard to control.

Capone proved so satisfactory to Torrio that by 1922, the older man made him number two in his organization. Before long, Capone was making about twenty-five thousand dollars a year (at a time when an ordinary working man made about one thousand dollars annually). With his money, he purchased a redbrick, two-story home on Prairie Avenue in the Chicago suburbs and brought his family from New York. The new household included Mae, Sonny, Teresa, Frank, John, Albert, Matthew, and Mafalda. Ralph, who had married, took an apartment in town, but he, too, could often be found visiting the family. "Al's a good boy,"[24] Teresa observed, happy that her son was caring for them.

Having ensured Capone's loyalty and reliability, Torrio gave him a variety of more important jobs, from purchasing trucks for the growing illegal liquor trade, to intimidating rivals. Recognizing that Capone had the intelligence and cunning to go far in the organization, Torrio also tried to teach his underling "the value of a bland smile and ready

The Beer War

By 1923, Chicago's Mayor Bill Thompson (who served from 1915 to 1923 and again from 1927 to 1931) had been dubbed by one reporter "the bad breath of Chicago politics."[25] City hall was overrun by gangsters and crooked officials. Prohibition was not being enforced. And as a result of corruption, the city was millions of dollars in debt.

In an attempt to clean up the problem, Chicago residents elected William E. "Decent" Dever to be the city's new mayor. Dever, a former Chicago councilman and judge, was a hardworking

Capone's home on South Prairie Avenue in Chicago.

man whose name had never been touched by scandal. Under him, police cracked down on crime. Many corrupt politicians lost power. Gang leaders did not know what their future would hold. Many worried that they would go to jail.

To one group of criminals, the Spike O'Donnell gang, the arrests motivated them to try to expand their liquor territory. They cut their prices lower than Torrio's and began forcing his customers to change their liquor supplier. One night they attacked six speakeasies that bought beer from Torrio and Capone, smashing furniture, beating up bystanders, and fracturing the skull of one of the owners.

Capone would not allow O'Donnell to get away with such activity. While O'Donnell's gangsters were at the last speakeasy, Capone's men burst in with guns blazing. One of O'Donnell's men was killed by a shotgun blast to the head. Ten days later, two more members of the O'Donnell gang were shot. Only one was lucky enough to survive.

Capone went on to set up further attacks during which O'Donnell's men were killed. Beer runner Phil Corrigan was shotgunned behind the wheel of his truck. Walter O'Donnell, Spike's brother, died in a gunfight. Even Spike O'Donnell himself was almost killed. The pressure eventually proved to be too much. O'Donnell decided to leave town. "Life with me is just one bullet after another,"[26] he said.

Move to the Suburbs

Despite their success in subduing O'Donnell, Torrio and Capone realized that Mayor Dever's cleanup campaign made it difficult and expensive for them to operate in Chicago. In late 1923, Torrio told Capone to find a location in the Chicago suburbs, beyond the reach of Dever's police, where they could set up new headquarters. Capone settled on the suburb of Cicero on Chicago's western border, home of sixty thousand working-class citizens, most of them immigrants from central Europe.

When Capone opened a house of prostitution in the neighborhood, however, a local named Eddie Vogel who controlled gambling in the community realized that his power could be threatened if the organization moved in. He told the Cicero police to raid the brothel and arrest all the girls. Torrio and Capone quickly made it clear to Vogel that, if he was wise and wanted to retain his income derived from gambling, he should allow them to stay. Torrio also asked the county sheriff, a friend of his, to shut down Vogel's gambling establishments. Vogel got the point—Torrio and Capone had too much clout to be stopped.

Certain that Vogel would not cause them further problems, Torrio and Capone needed to find someone to work as a liaison between their organization and community merchants, bankers, and lesser politicians. Frank

John Torrio, Capone's mentor and the founder of the mobster association known as "the organization."

local journalist later observed, "The Capones owned the whole town, from the street corner to every desk at city hall and police stations. It was an invasion and they just took over."[28]

Al soon set up headquarters in Cicero, first in a modest redbrick building known as Anton's Hotel, then later in the nearby Hawthorne Inn. Torrio owned the latter, so Capone renovated it to ensure his own safety, which included having bulletproof steel shutters installed on the windows. He also stationed armed bodyguards at all strategic locations. A reporter recalled, "There were never fewer than a dozen . . . idlers in the lobby—fellows with . . . eyes as expressionless as those of a dead mackerel; the Capone bodyguard. They gazed from behind newspapers and through a haze of cigarette smoke amid a silence that was earsplitting."[29]

Capone seemed to be the perfect choice. He was polished and persuasive. He also had a reputation of being a cold-blooded murderer. One of his favorite sayings was, "You don't get no back talk from a corpse."[27]

With Frank to persuade, intimidate, and make payoffs, the further establishment of nightclubs and gambling dens in Cicero was easy. One

Rest in Peace, Frank Capone

Content that Al Capone was able to handle his affairs, Torrio decided to take a vacation in Italy. Capone continued to work to expand the organization's power, but without his mentor's levelheaded influence, he was more inclined to use violence to achieve his ends. A glaring display of this occurred during Cicero's mayoral elections in April 1924. Capone, who supported the corrupt incumbent candidate, sent his men to destroy the office of the opposition. Then, on election day, Capone's thugs cruised the streets, harassing voters. One election clerk was kidnapped; a policeman was assaulted; and four people were killed. An observer reported:

> As a voter waited in line to cast his ballot, a menacing, slouch-hatted figure would sidle up to him and ask how he intended to vote. If the reply was unsatisfactory, the hooligan would snatch the ballot from him, mark it himself, hand it back, and stand by, fingering the revolver in his coat pocket, until the voter had dropped the ballot into the box.[30]

Before the day was over, however, Capone learned that intimidation sometimes had its price. Because of the violence, a group of plainclothes police in unmarked cars had been called from Chicago to help keep order. Near dusk, as they neared a Cicero polling place, they recognized Frank Capone on the sidewalk. It is unclear whether Frank mistook them for rival gang members or not, but as the officers got out of their cars and walked toward him, he reached for his gun. The police began shooting, and when they stopped, Frank lay dead on the street.

Al Capone was grief-stricken and spared no expense when it came to his brother's funeral. It was one of the grandest the city of Chicago had ever seen. Frank's coffin was silver plated and satin lined. Flowers spilled out over the front porch of the Capone home and festooned the lampposts. The crowd of mourners in the funeral procession stretched for blocks. The *Chicago Tribune* reported, "Dressed in their best, bringing their womenfolk, . . . the kings, princes, nobility, and commonality of the underworld gathered in hundreds yesterday to pay their last respects to their late brother in arms, Frank Caponi [Capone]."[31]

End of a Troublemaker

John Torrio was one of those who grieved the loss of Frank Capone. Torrio returned from Italy about the time of the Cicero elections. Despite the tragedy, he was pleased to find that Capone had successfully established at least 120 illegal saloons in Cicero, along with nightclubs and gambling joints. Mindful of what he owed the young man, in 1924 he made him a fifty-fifty partner in the organization.

There were those in Cicero who were not grateful for Capone's takeover of the suburb, however. One of the most persistent and outspoken was Robert St. John, owner of the *Cicero Tribune*, a small weekly newspaper. Beginning in 1922, St. John began attacking Torrio and Capone and

Lost Cause

Editor Robert St. John was not the only upstanding citizen to oppose Capone. The Reverend Henry C. Hoover and a group of concerned citizens who called themselves the West Suburban Citizens' Association were dedicated to combating gangsterism in the Chicago suburbs. But, as John Kobler describes in Capone: The Life and World of Al Capone, *they were not prepared to resist the gangster's violent retaliation.*

On May 16, 1925, having badgered a reluctant Sheriff Hoffman into taking action against the Hawthorne Smoke Shop [a Cicero gambling den], the minister [Hoover] accompanied . . . a token force of deputy sheriffs, reinforced by the association's most militant members. . . . Presently, Capone, who had spent the night at the Hawthorne Inn next door, elbowed his way through the crowd. . . .

"Reverend," he said, "can't you and I get together—come to some understanding?" The minister asked what he meant. "If you'll let up on me in Cicero," Capone explained, "I'll withdraw from Stickney [another Chicago suburb]."

"Mr. Capone," said Hoover, "the only understanding you and I can have is that you must obey the law or get out of the western suburbs."

The raiders did not leave the scene unscathed. Capone's thugs who had been mingling with the crowd outside, broke [committee member Chester] Bragg's nose with a blackjack. They threw [David] Morgan to the ground and kicked him in the face. . . .

Rather than expose its members to further reprisals, the Citizens' Association decided to participate in no more raids. . . . The Hawthorne Smoke Shop underwent no radical change. Half an hour after the raid new gambling equipment and cash reserves had been moved in, and by nightfall it was operating again at full tilt.

exposing their criminal activities in print. Capone at first tried to put the paper out of business by pressuring merchants not to advertise. He also tried threats, to both St. John and his staff. "[Capone henchmen] harassed my reporters almost immediately, either bribed them or threatened them. There were frequent telephone threats.

I had a big turnover of reporters,"[32] St. John remembered.

The threats did not work, though, so Capone resorted to violence and then bribery. In 1925, three of his men stopped the publisher on his way to work and beat him with their gun butts. When St. John was discharged from the hospital, he went down to the police station and asked for Capone's arrest. To St. John's puzzlement, he was told by the police to return the next morning at 9:00 A.M. The journalist returned on schedule, and was shown to a private office where a well-dressed man with a scar on his left cheek awaited him. It was Capone. He first apologized for his men's assault on St. John. Then he produced a thick wad of money. Realizing that Capone wanted to buy his support, St. John turned and left the room.

His uncompromising spirit was admirable, but St. John found that it was hard to beat Capone. Several days later, he discovered that Capone had pressured the *Tribune*'s investors into selling him their shares of the paper. Capone was now St. John's boss. "I guess you and your scar-faced friend have won," the editor told the

The Sieben Brewery in Chicago, the scene of a 1924 police raid that ended in the arrest of mobster John Torrio.

messenger who gave him the news. "Say good-bye to him for me."[33]

That day, St. John left Cicero forever. He later became a distinguished foreign correspondent and broadcaster.

Cold-Blooded Murder

As the St. John incident proved, Torrio and Capone did not hesitate to use brute force to make people do what they wanted. That fact was emphasized with the murder of Dion O'Banion. O'Banion, a florist with a reputation for having killed at least twenty-five men, was an unreliable ally of Torrio. "He [O'Banion] was an indefatigable [tireless] handshaker and backslapper, though never at the same time; at least one hand stayed free to go for one of the three gun pockets tailored into his clothes,"[34] said one observer.

In May 1924, O'Banion learned that one of his holdings, the Sieben Brewery, was going to be raided and shut down by the police. Slyly, he went to Torrio, who was a joint owner of the brewery, offering to sell his share for half a million dollars. Torrio agreed to pay. When he arrived at the brewery to oversee the arrival of a shipment, however, federal agents stormed in and arrested him. There was no doubt in Torrio's mind that he had been double-crossed. O'Banion even bragged about how he had tricked his former partner, and flatly refused to return Torrio's money.

Torrio and Capone decided that they could no longer trust O'Banion,

and they decided to eliminate him. On November 10, 1924, as O'Banion worked in his florist shop filling the day's orders, three strangers entered. Two of them were hit men named John Scalise and Albert Anselmi. The other is unknown but may have been Frankie Yale. As O'Banion extended his hand in greeting, Yale gripped it tightly. Scalise and Anselmi pulled out their guns. Five shots rang out, striking O'Banion in the face and chest. He fell dead among the ferns and chrysanthemums.

Terrible Revenge

Although the police rounded up the usual suspects (including Capone and Torrio) after O'Banion's death, they could find no evidence to make arrests. On the other hand, Hymie Weiss, a friend of O'Banion, did not need hard evidence to decide who was responsible for the murder. He vowed revenge on Capone and Torrio.

Learning of his danger, Torrio and his wife left town for an extended vacation. Capone, however, remained in Chicago to take his chances. He soon discovered that Weiss was serious in his threat. On one occasion, Capone's car was forced off the road and raked with machine gun bullets. He was not in the car, but he recognized that he could easily have been killed. A short time later, Weiss's men kidnapped Capone's chauffeur and tortured the man to death in an attempt to learn details of Capone's daily routine.

In response, Capone increased his security precautions. He never went anywhere without at least two bodyguards. He ordered a specially built Cadillac sedan with a seven-ton steel-armored body and bulletproof glass windows. He used only a trusted man as a chauffeur, and directed one carload of bodyguards to precede him and one to follow whenever he went out driving. At home he never stood or sat near a window, and usually kept the

Capone's specially constructed Cadillac featured steel lining, bulletproof windows, and a large motor capable of doing 110 miles per hour.

A Cadillac for the Big Fellow

Al Capone was colorful and captivating, even in the measures he took to protect himself from danger. So strong was his charisma that even one of America's most respected businesses, automobile manufacturer General Motors, found itself overlooking his dark side in favor of the profit and prestige they could garner. Historian Geoffrey Perrett explains in his book America in the Twenties: A History.

Capone's larger-than-life personality filled the newspapers day after day. And that was new for a crime boss. Capone cultivated the press as if he were running for office. A Capone mobster could be identified (when not working undercover, as it were) by his pearl gray felt hat, a narrow band of black silk circling the crown. The Twenties saw color return to men's clothing after a century of increasing drabness, and Capone in his lime-green suits and silk ties of dazzling hue was a peacock. General Motors . . . was perfectly happy to build a special Cadillac for the Big Fellow, seven tons in weight, with an armor-plated body, steel-encased gas tank, bullet-proof glass half an inch thick, and a special compartment behind the rear seat for carrying guns. The windows were designed so that those inside the car could shoot at pursuers without exposing themselves unduly. It was obviously a gangster's car, its design made sense only in one context for a private citizen—the commission of crime. GM did not even pause to consider the matter. They simply sent in their bill for $30,000.

shades drawn in case of snipers. As one historian wrote, "For him, security, constant vigilance, and bodyguards were neither an encumbrance nor an admission of cowardice, they were a way of life."[35]

Torrio, when he returned to Chicago, was not so cautious. He went back to his usual routine, without bodyguards or guns. It proved to be a mistake. On January 12, 1925, just before dusk, he and his wife returned home from a shopping trip. As Ann Torrio walked to the front door, John Torrio gathered up their boxes and packages. He did not immediately notice a car that slowly pulled up beside him. When he did see the four armed men inside, escape was impossible.

Torrio ran toward his house, but two of the men, Hymie Weiss and a thug named "Bugs" Moran, jumped out of the car and opened fire. Torrio was hit in the chest and the neck and fell to the sidewalk. Weiss and Moran shot him again in the right arm and the groin. Moran then aimed the gun at Torrio's head. The gun was out of bullets, though, and an approaching laundry van caused the men to flee. Torrio's wife dragged her husband into the house and called an ambulance. When later asked if he had recognized his attackers, Torrio muttered, "Sure, I know all four men, but I'll never tell their names."[36] He kept his promise.

As Torrio recovered, watched over by Al Capone who slept in his hospital room, he realized that he had been seriously mistaken to think that he could live like a legitimate businessman and still be involved in crime. Danger was unavoidable, and he did not want to risk his life or his family's lives any longer. It was time to place his organization in the hands of a young, energetic colleague who had the ruthlessness and ambition to get the better of his enemies. There was only one man he could think of who would fit the bill: Al Capone.

Chapter Three

"There Goes Al!"

Despite the severity of his wounds, after four weeks John Torrio was well enough to attend the trial stemming from his arrest at the Sieben Brewery. He was convicted and sentenced to nine months in the Lake County prison in northeastern Illinois. Thanks to his money and influence, he passed the time behind bars in relative comfort, housed in a private cell that he decorated with Oriental rugs and good furniture.

Despite these comforts, Torrio did not change his mind about leaving the Chicago organization behind. In March 1925, Torrio summoned Capone to prison and announced that he was retiring. Since Al, Ralph, Matthew, and Albert had all worked for him in one capacity or another, Torrio turned over the organization to the entire Capone family.

Head Man

Suddenly, Al Capone found himself the head of a vast crime empire. He controlled nightclubs, gambling establishments, breweries, speakeasies, and brothels. He was also responsible for smuggling and bootlegging operations, paying off police and other public officials, maintaining security for himself and his henchmen, and dealing with the menace of his rivals.

To run such a massive enterprise, Capone needed reliable assistance, and he knew the right men to choose. His loyal and hardworking business manager was former pimp Jack "Greasy Thumb" Guzik, who also made payoffs to Chicago police and politicians. Brother Ralph Capone became director of liquor sales. A trusted associate, Lewis Cowan, was the organization's bondsman, ready in a minute to post bail for anyone who was arrested.

For protection, Capone retained an assortment of sharpshooters, muscle men, and bodyguards such as "Machine Gun" Jack McGurn, and Phil D'Andrea, who reportedly could split a quarter in midair using a rifle. Capone also had reliable managers to oversee his prostitution and gambling operations, the collection of protection

Capone's business manager Jack Guzik.

money and bets, and other criminal ventures. Tony Berardi, a photographer for the *Chicago Evening American* said of Capone's talents:

> He [Capone] was no dummy. He knew how to pick people for certain positions in certain categories. He had people who met with the mayor, with the chief of police, and so on. And they were not all Italians. He had people of every nationality you could think of.[37]

Twisted Celebrity

John Torrio had always chosen to keep a low profile, not wanting to attract attention to his illegal activities, but Al Capone was different. First he moved his main headquarters from the Hawthorne Inn in Cicero to a suite of rooms in the Metropole Hotel in downtown Chicago. "From the moment Al Capone moved to the Metropole, all Chicago was aware of his presence," writes one of his biographers. "It was as visible an address as there was in the city."[38]

Capone made himself visible in other ways as well. He dressed well wherever he went, earning the nickname "Snorky," or stylish, from his friends. He wore expensive, brightly colored suits (his favorites were green and canary yellow). His shirts were custom-made and monogrammed. An 11.5-carat diamond ring twinkled on his finger. As he rode down the

"Machine Gun" Jack McGurn was one of Capone's many bodyguards.

Chicago streets in his Cadillac, trailing carloads of bodyguards, people lined the curb hoping to get a glimpse of him. "There goes Al!"[39] they would cry.

One of Capone's favorite pastimes was driving to city hall where he walked up and down the street, stopping to talk to officials who were on his payroll. He also enjoyed attending the theater, prizefights, and baseball games, where he could be found smiling and shaking hands with the crowd. He was a regular at the track, and, as a

compulsive gambler, sometimes bet up to $100,000 on a horse or a dog race. He often lost more than he won, sometimes losing $200,000 in an evening. He took his losses philosophically, however, and witnesses claimed that he always paid what he owed. Later in his career he estimated he had squandered more than $7 million since 1920, much of it attributed to gambling losses.

Capone liked to use reporters and photographers to help promote an image of himself as a "good guy" with nothing to hide. Aware that his remarks would be quoted, he talked to them as if he were a misunderstood businessman. Sometimes he acted as if he were a public benefactor. At other times, he came across as an ordinary person, with problems just like the average workingman. Says one journalist, "The press made Al Capone into a real character, a human being that people could have an image of. . . . He was the first gangster who gave newspapers the chance to really portray the people, the individuals, who chose to lead the life of organized crime."[40]

Perhaps because they felt that they knew him, most of the public did not fear Al Capone. He habitually treated decent, law-abiding people with respect. "He always tipped his hat to us and he was always polite,"[41] remembered one woman. His politeness even extended to some policemen, to whom he would wave and smile if he saw them on the street. "I got nothing against the honest cop on the beat,"[42] he insisted. Indeed, to many people the most notorious gangster of the age appeared to be just a generous, if slightly crooked, businessman, a friendly bootlegger at a time when many people disliked Prohibition.

The Adonis Club Massacre

The public would have been shocked to see the other side of Capone, however.

Capone attends a Chicago football game in 1931 wearing his signature bent fedora and camel's hair coat. Unlike other gangsters, Capone enjoyed being seen in public.

Like Torrio, he never hesitated to use force if it served his purposes, and by the end of 1929, he and his gang were credited with more than three hundred murders in the Chicago area.

One instance of his brutality occurred in December 1925, when he took his wife and son to New York to seek treatment for Sonny's chronic ear infections. While they were there, Capone met with his old friend Frankie Yale to work out a liquor smuggling transaction. Yale invited Capone to a Christmas Day party at a Brooklyn speakeasy called the Adonis Social and Athletic Club, and Capone accepted.

Shortly before the festivities began, Yale learned that a rival New York gangster, Richard "Peg-Leg" Lonergan, was going to crash the party and cause trouble. Yale suggested that they cancel the get-together, but Capone had another idea: they could prepare a surprise attack for Lonergan and his men.

About three in the morning, as the party was in full swing, Lonergan and his men arrived. Yale let them enter, and they pushed their way to the bar, all the while making loud and obnoxious comments. They did not recognize Capone and his men, who were sitting at a table near the back. A short time later, Capone gave a nod, a prearranged signal, and the lights went out. Then he and his men pulled out guns, and bullets began to fly. "Chairs and tables toppled over; glassware shattered; screams rent the air as the customers piled hatless and coatless into the street,"[43] wrote one historian.

When the police arrived a few minutes later, the club was dark and silent. Exploring it by flashlight, they discovered the remains of the shootout. At least three of Lonergan's men had been killed. Lonergan himself had died so quickly that his gun was still in its shoulder holster. The police rounded up several Adonis employees and the few of Lonergan's gang who survived, but they could find no one willing to testify about what happened.

A few days later, Capone gathered up his family and returned to Chicago. He was pleased that he had been able to display his city's gang power over that of New York. "Chicago is the imperial city of the gang world, and New York a remote provincial place,"[44] wrote one journalist for the *New Yorker* magazine shortly thereafter.

Death of the "Hanging Prosecutor"

The incident at the Adonis Club was a Capone triumph. Another killing later that spring, that of assistant state attorney William Harold McSwiggin, was a disaster. Twenty-six-year-old McSwiggin was a well-liked political figure in Chicago. He was unmarried and lived with his parents and four sisters. His father was a respected Chicago policeman. McSwiggin, nicknamed the "hanging prosecutor," was a hard worker with a reputation for winning difficult cases.

Despite his reputation, however, McSwiggin had ties to Chicago's crime world. Specifically, he was a longtime friend of brothers Myles and William "Klondike" O'Donnell, rivals of Capone. McSwiggin made a habit of going out with them to various speakeasies and restaurants for a few hours of fun.

On the night of April 27, 1926, McSwiggin went out with Myles O'Donnell and some friends, allegedly to find a card game they could join. Late that evening, Capone learned that the O'Donnell car had been spotted in his territory. Since the brothers had lately been trying to interfere with his bootleg operations, Capone considered this an act of provocation. Determined to teach his rivals a lesson, Capone and his men piled into several cars and sped off in search of the tresspassers. He soon came across their vehicle, parked in front of the Pony Inn, a tavern in Cicero.

Seeing O'Donnell and several others in front of the tavern, Capone and his men opened fire. They did not realize, however, that McSwiggin was a part of the group. Caught in a spray of bullets, McSwiggin and a gangster named Jim Doherty were killed instantly.

Repercussions

McSwiggin's murder had been a mistake. He had simply been in the wrong

place at the wrong time. And although people wondered what a public prosecutor was doing riding around with known gangsters, his death caused a widespread outcry against Chicago's crime problem. Frightened that outlaws did not always confine their killing to each other, the citizens of Chicago demanded that something be done.

Law enforcement responded. "It will be a war to the hilt against these gangsters,"[45] announced state attorney Robert E. Crowe, who had been McSwiggin's boss. He ordered police to arrest every hoodlum they could find—specifically Al Capone, who was the chief suspect. Deputies raided saloons, speakeasies, brothels, and gambling houses. These included twenty-five of Al Capone's properties such as the Hawthorne Smoke Shop in Cicero and the Stockade, a brothel in nearby Forest View. In a punishing frenzy, raiders smashed slot machines, arrested prostitutes, and hauled away safes full of cash. A group of irate citizens even set fire to the Stockade; firefighters just stood around and watched it burn. "Why don't you do something?" a Capone employee begged. "Can't spare the water,"[46] a fireman replied.

In Hiding

The furor aroused by McSwiggin's murder forced Al Capone to go into hiding for several months. In great secrecy, he went west to Lansing, Michigan, where he took shelter at the

Friend and Benefactor

After the death of William McSwiggin, Al Capone fled to the midwestern town of Lansing, Michigan. There he lived the life of an ordinary American and, as Laurence Bergreen details in Capone: The Man and His Era, *successfully convinced Lansing residents that he did not deserve his reputation as a bad man.*

The Al Capone the Italians of Lansing came to know was nothing like the 'Scarface' whose evil deeds regularly made headlines in the Chicago dailies. When the people of Lansing considered Capone, they did not think of beer wars, drive-by machine-gun shootings, and a rat's nest of urban corruption. They did not shudder at the thought of a powerful racketeering organization dealing in vice and death. The Al Capone they knew in Lansing was a soft-spoken, impeccably groomed man burdened by concerns about which he rarely spoke and given to intoxicating bursts of charity. To them, he was neither a pimp, gambler, murderer, or racketeer. He was a friend, a benefactor, and in some cases a savior. . . . In Lansing, he could walk the streets without fearing for his life; here, if nowhere else, men were not out to kill him, and the knowledge that one such refuge existed made him feel human and offered a measure of redemption from the corruption and violence he had sown in Chicago.

home of a friend, a former racketeer from Chicago.

The period was a welcome break from the strains of criminal life. During his stay in Lansing, Capone lived as a law-abiding citizen. He kept a low profile and caused no trouble. With his easygoing, ingratiating manner, he made many friends, including Lansing's chief of police, who, risking his career, kept the gangster's presence in the area a secret.

Far from dangerous rivals and free from police harassment, Capone had a relatively carefree summer. He went quietly around town, shopping and exchanging greetings with passersby on the streets. He rented a lakeside cabin outside of town and spent hours swimming and lying in the sun. He met a pretty young woman and started an affair. One of his friends described her as a "beautiful gal, as nice as you can be and still be involved with that group. Al met her in the roadhouse."[47]

Capone, the Peacemaker

After several months in Lansing, Capone was ready to return to Chicago. He contacted law enforcement officials there, and offered to meet them and face their accusations in the McSwiggin murder. "I think the time is ripe for me to prove my innocence of the charges that have been made against me. I've been convicted without a hearing of all the crimes on the calendar. But I'm innocent, and it won't take long to prove it,"[48] he told a reporter in late July.

He was right. His lawyer Thomas Nash had the reputation of knowing who to bribe or threaten in order to get his clients off, and he proved helpful to Capone. Shortly after everyone convened in court on July 29, 1926, a judge dismissed the McSwiggin case, citing that there was not enough evidence to prove Capone's involvement.

Capone's exoneration bolstered his opinion of himself. His ego swelled, and he began to talk about how many people he helped (by employing them in his criminal enterprises) and about how generous he was to those in need. He claimed that he yearned for peace with his rivals, and even went so far as to set up a "peace conference" of all the most powerful gangsters in Chicago. His avowed purpose was to formally divide up the city among leading gangs in order to reduce the competition and killing.

On October 20, 1926, in a much-publicized meeting, Capone and a few of his men met with a group that included Bugs Moran, Klondike and Myles O'Donnell, Maxie Eisen, and several others. One journalist wrote,

There they sat, thieves, highwaymen, . . . murderers, ex-convicts, thugs, and hoodlums—human beasts of prey, once skulking in holes as dark as the sewers of Paris, now come out in the open. . . . Here they sat, partitioning Chicago and Cook County into trade areas, . . . going about it with the assurance of a group of directors of United States Steel.[49]

Capone proposed a five-point treaty: Everyone would agree to forget and

Mug shot of gangster and Capone rival Bugs Moran.

forgive all former feuds. All would renounce violence as a means of settling disputes. There would be no more gossip about rival members. There would be no more stealing of each other's customers or encroaching on established territories. Violations within a gang would be punished by that gang's headman.

Capone also laid out new boundaries for all the gangs, taking care to keep control of a large part of Chicago and the suburbs for himself. "Just like the old days," he told a reporter. "They (the O'Banion gang) stay on the North Side and I stay in Cicero and if we meet on the street, we say 'hello' and shake hands. Better, ain't it?"[50] His rivals decided to accept the terms. Capone was so powerful he could get anything he wanted.

Influential and Well-to-Do

For a time, Chicago's underworld was more peaceful and profitable. With

Plea for Peace

In October 1926, Capone summoned the press to Chicago's Hawthorne Hotel for an informal press conference. There, he met them with a picture of his son in his hand and explained the reasons he wanted to make peace with Chicago's other gangsters. Robert Schoenberg includes the incident and Capone's remarks in Mr. Capone: The Real—And Complete—Story of Al Capone.

"I've got a boy," Capone said, showing the reporters Sonny's picture. "I love the kid more than anything in the world and next to him I love his mother and then my own mother and my sisters and brothers," he said. "And it's pretty terrible, too, when you think I have not been able to go home to my wife and boy for fourteen months."

"I don't want to die. Especially I don't want to die in the street, punctured with machine gun fire."

"That's the reason I've asked for peace. I've begged those fellows to put away their pistols and talk sense. They've all got families too. Most of them are kids and haven't got any children of their own, but they've got mothers and sisters."

"What makes them so crazy to end up on a slab in a morgue, with their mothers' hearts broken over the way they died, I don't know. I've tried to find out but I can't. I know I've tried since the first pistol was drawn in this fight to show them that there's enough business for all of us without killing each other like animals in the street. Competition needn't be a matter of murder, anyway. But they don't see it."

In its glory days the Lexington Hotel served as Capone's home and headquarters. However, it was demolished shortly after this 1995 picture.

Capone's help, Big Bill Thompson was reelected mayor in 1927. His return to office marked even greater prosperity for criminals. As if to celebrate, Capone himself enlarged his offices at the Metropole Hotel, taking over more than fifty rooms. Prostitutes came and went, gambling flourished, and liquor was available at any time. In 1928, he moved across the street to the more imposing Lexington Hotel and set up similar accommodations there.

By 1928, the illegal liquor trade was a major source of Capone's $100 million-a-year income, bringing in an estimated $60 million annually. Because Prohibition was becoming so unpopular throughout the nation, though, he guessed that the law would soon be repealed. Thus he expanded his organization to put more emphasis on racketeering. Eventually he and his partners controlled almost three-quarters of the Chicago rackets that ruled such businesses as automobile mechanics, distilled water dealers, florists, carpet layers, and a host of others. From them alone, Capone made an estimated $10 million annually. Bribes and payoffs cut heavily into his profits, though. By 1929, he claimed that he paid $30 million annually for police and political protection.

With so many enterprises to oversee, Al Capone spent his days like the president of a prosperous business, making decisions and dealing with administrative details. Sunday was his busiest, because lawyers, judges, and politicians visited then to ask for favors. He received them in his office, seated at his desk, with portraits of George Washington, Abraham Lincoln, and Big Bill Thompson on the wall behind him.

One of the most notable favors ever asked of Capone was a police request that he be present to greet Italian pilot Francesco de Pinedo when de Pinedo arrived in Chicago. The pilot was a representative of controversial Italian fascist leader Benito Mussolini. The police believed that Capone's presence would prevent possible antifascist demonstrations more effectively than squads of their own men. Capone agreed to be part of the welcoming party made up of city officials, and was one of the first to shake de Pinedo's hand after he landed.

In another instance, Frank J. Loesch, head of the Chicago Crime Commission, the city's primary anti-crime organization, asked the gang

leader to use his influence to help ensure peaceful and honest city elections in 1928. Capone agreed to keep everyone in line. Loesch remembered, "It turned out to be the squarest and the most successful election day in forty years. There was not one complaint, not one election fraud and no threat of trouble all day."[51]

St. Valentine's Day

No matter how polished and businesslike Capone tried to be, an aura of violence hung about him. At times, his brutality was unspeakable. In July 1928, for example, he ordered the assassination of his old friend and employer Frankie Yale. Yale had been instrumental in Capone's success, but had become friendly with one of Capone's rivals. Capone also suspected that Yale was behind hijackings of his liquor shipments between New York and Chicago.

In the weeks after the killing, police tracked Yale's killers to Chicago and guessed that Capone had arranged for the shooting. But the gang leader had an alibi—he had been in Miami, Florida, at the time—so the police were unable to make an arrest.

Capone was also in Florida for one of the most infamous gang killings of the 1920s, the St. Valentine's Day Massacre of 1929. Again, no proof existed that Capone was involved, but he was a top suspect because the murderers appeared to have been targeting

Jazz Age Sheik

As he rose to power, Capone surrounded himself with a variety of tough, loyal men who would not hesitate to kill for him if necessary. Jack McGurn was one of the toughest, and as John Kobler points out in Capone: The Life and World of Al Capone, *also one of the most stylish.*

Capone valued none of his young recruits more highly than Jack McGurn—'Machine Gun' Jack McGurn, as he was called after the tommy gun became his preferred weapon. He was born Vincenzo De Mora in Little Italy to one of the Gennas' alky [alcohol] cookers, who died full of buckshot following his sale of some alcohol to the competition. The son, according to legend, determined to avenge the murder, began practicing marksmanship by shooting the sparrows off telephone wires with a Daisy repeating rifle....

McGurn was the complete jazz age sheik [modern young man], a ukulele strummer, cabaret habitué [frequenter of nightclubs] and snaky dancer. An insatiable collector of women, preferably blondes, he parted his curly black hair in the middle and slicked it down with pomade until it lay as flat and sleek as [1920s actor] Rudolph Valentino's. He wore wide-checked suits heavily padded in the shoulders, flower-figured neckties and pointed patent-leather shoes. The police ascribed twenty-two murders to McGurn, five of them supposedly committed in reprisal for his father's death. As a gesture of contempt after mowing down a victim, he would sometimes press a nickel into his hand.

"Machine Gun" Jack McGurn and his wife Louise Rolf.

one of his most troublesome rivals, Bugs Moran.

Moran had assumed leadership of Dion O'Banion's gang after Hymie Weiss's death in October 1926, and Capone had tolerated Moran's hostility for a long time. Moran had taken part in the attempted murder of John Torrio in 1925, and had tried to kill Capone in 1926. Moran had also twice tried to kill one of Capone's favorite bodyguards, "Machine Gun" Jack McGurn. Thus, when McGurn came to Capone with a plan to eliminate the troublemaker, Capone gave him permission to act.

McGurn's plan was creative. He would lure Moran and his men to a garage to buy a shipment of bootleg liquor. When they were inside, hit men dressed in stolen police uniforms would appear, as though they were raiding the place. The victims would be caught off guard and would thus be easier to murder.

The plan worked well. On February 14, 1929, seven members of Moran's gang arrived at the garage. A few minutes later, another car pulled up. Four men, two of them dressed as police, got out and entered the garage. Gangsters usually tried to appear law-abiding when confronted by the police, so when Moran's men saw the uniformed newcomers, they obeyed orders, laid down their guns, and faced the wall. With their backs turned, they could not see McGurn's men produce submachine guns from under their coats. McGurn's men mowed down Moran's seven, and then got back in their car and drove away. Moran was not murdered, however, because he was late for the meeting.

Officials who investigated the killings found that McGurn had an alibi, a blond beauty named Louise Rolf, who testified that she and McGurn had spent the day together. The murders were never officially solved, but Moran himself named the person responsible. "Only Capone kills like that!"[52] he said, referring to the efficiency and brutality of the crime.

Murder for Dinner

As the St. Valentine's massacre demonstrated, Capone allowed others to do his killing for him. There was less risk of his getting caught that way. At times, however, he believed that a personal show of force was essential. Capone's murder of two of his own hit men, John Scalise and Albert Anselmi, was an example of this.

In the spring of 1929, Scalise and Anselmi, who had worked for the Genna gang and then Capone since their arrival in America about 1920, yielded to the persuasions of a rival gang leader, Joseph Guinta. For fifty thousand dollars, the two men agreed to betray Capone and murder him. Before they could act, however, Capone learned of the plan. He invited the unsuspecting three to a banquet, where he provided plenty of wine and

A crowd gathers outside a Chicago warehouse as police remove the unwitting victims of a Capone crime.

brandy along with an excellent dinner. Then, when all were relaxed and full, Capone picked up a baseball bat and unleashed his anger.

He battered the three unmercifully, not stopping until he had broken nearly every bone in their bodies. "Capone got so worked up they thought he had a heart attack,"[53] recalled one of his

men. Scalise, Anselmi, and Guinta were then shot and their bodies driven out to the country and dumped.

"I'm Human"

After such a performance, it is hard to believe that Capone was anything but a villain, and many who learned of the incident considered him such. He protested the label, however, insisting, "I'm not as black as I'm painted. I'm human. I've got a heart in me."[54]

Capone did have a human side, despite what most of the world believed. "He fed many and many a bum," one friend testified. "I don't know what he gained by being kind to those kind of people because they couldn't do anything for him; he was doing it for them. But that's the kind of individual he was. He just liked people."[55]

Whether Capone was a people lover, or a shrewd businessman who periodically tried to restore his public image, no one could say for sure. There was no arguing, however, that his shameless flamboyance and defiance of the law elevated him to a level of notoriety that few criminals attained before or since.

Chapter Four

FAMILY MAN

In contrast to Al Capone's lawless and unconventional career, his home life closely paralleled that of other Italian Americans. He appreciated good friends, good food, and good music. As the most successful member of his large family, he willingly took responsibility for his siblings, mother, wife, and son. In 1929, his sister Mafalda Capone told reporters, "If people only knew him as I know him, they would not say the things about him they do. I adore him. And he is his mother's life. He is so very good, so kind to us. You who only know him from the newspaper stories will never realize the real man he is."[56]

Women in Their Place

Mafalda Capone had valid reason to believe her older brother was kind and good. Like many other members of the underworld, Al Capone compartmentalized his life, keeping his home life entirely separate from his criminal existence. Teresa, Mae, and Mafalda were never exposed to the brutal side of his business. Rather, they saw him only as an indulgent son, husband, and brother who protected them from unpleasantness and did not discuss his work affairs with them.

None of the women asked Capone about what he did when he left the house. Mae did not inquire about people who visited their home. She did not ask about Capone's whereabouts when he was gone for weeks at a time. Instead, she was content to concentrate on home and family and to enjoy the many luxuries that her husband lavished on her. As one historian writes,

Here Comes the Bride

Throughout his life, Capone took great pride in providing for his family, and when the time came for his sister Mafalda to marry, he spent extravagantly to make the day unforgettable. Historian Laurence Bergreen details the event in Capone: The Man and His Era.

Chicago had witnessed many opulent gangster funerals over the last ten years, but nothing equaled the splendor of Mafalda's nuptial ceremony. The bride wore an ivory satin wedding gown, complete with a twenty-five-foot train. In her ample hands she grasped a bouquet comprised of 400 lilies. Five bridesmaids, wearing matching pink taffeta gowns and blue slippers, formed the wedding party. During the ceremony, an organ played softly, but, according to one account, "there was an air of furtive [secretive] repression upon many within the edifice [building], and detectives, unbidden guests, quietly removed five uneasy men, each of whom was carrying a pistol." Ralph Capone, convicted tax evader, gave Mafalda away. As Mafalda left the church on the arm of her new husband, the mother of the bride, Teresa Capone, dwarfed in a mink coat, dabbed her eyes with a handkerchief. It had been a perfect afternoon, with one significant exception. Although the wedding guests and journalists alike looked for him everywhere, Al Capone, fearing arrest, was nowhere to be seen.

"Pale, bland, compliant, soft, and silent. Virtue on a pedestal towering over him. . . . A household goddess. That was just the way Al wanted his wife."[57]

Although Capone expected his wife to be virtuous and faithful, he was not. He was attracted to beautiful young women, and throughout his life he visited prostitutes and had affairs with women who caught his eye. In addition to the mistress he took during the summer he spent in Lansing, Michigan, he had at least four others throughout his lifetime, and rumor had it that he arranged for prostitutes and one of his girlfriends to visit him while he was in Cook County prison in 1931. Although Capone treated these women well, they came to see him only when they were invited, and they could make no demands on him. All understood that Capone's true loyalties lay with Mae and his family, and that he would not disrupt those ties.

Capone was also careful never to be seen with his mistresses in public, realizing that it would contradict the gentlemanly image he wanted to maintain. "I never saw him with a woman, nor did any other newspaperman. At least fifteen of us got together, and the subject came up, and not one of us ever saw Al Capone with a [mistress],"[58] remembers one journalist. Capone was also seldom seen in public with his wife, mother, or sister, because he was determined to protect their safety and anonymity.

Nothing But the Best

Despite his unfaithfulness—or perhaps because of it—Capone made sure that Mae and Sonny had the best of everything. In 1928, he purchased a large beachfront estate in Miami, Florida, and allowed Mae to furnish it as she desired. Among her many purchases were reproductions of antique furniture, gold-trimmed dinner services, a brass and enamel vanity set, ivory figurines, and a silver-plated juicer. One observer says, "Everywhere she went, she left a trail of thousand-dollar bills, to the delight of local merchants. To the extent that respectability could be bought, Mae did so, and she paid for it in cash."[59] Capone himself had an oversized swimming pool built on the

Capone's sprawling beachfront residence in Miami, Florida.

Capone and his son Sonny chat with Gaby Hartnett of the Chicago Cubs at a game. Sonny was seldom seen in public.

property and purchased two boats, which he used for fishing.

Sonny, Capone's only child, had everything money could buy as well. There was always an abundance of toys for him to play with, and when he wanted to invite some of his classmates to swim in the Capone pool in Miami, Capone threw a lavish party for more than fifty of them.

Sonny was Capone's pride and joy, but he was also a source of concern. He was a shy, sickly boy who suffered from serious ear infections when he was young. Capone, wanting the best care

for his son, took him to a New York specialist for surgery in 1925, and offered the doctor one hundred thousand dollars to treat the boy. The doctor assured him that his usual fee of one thousand dollars was sufficient, and the surgery was successful. Sonny's hearing was permanently damaged from the infections, however.

Capone also tried to ensure that his son was shielded from those who might try to harm him because he was a gangster's son. Sonny attended private school and seldom went out in public. Capone even sometimes used "stand-ins" for his son at public events such as baseball games. Because of his sheltered life, Sonny had a safe childhood.

The Good Son

Capone's care for Teresa Capone throughout his life was also exceptional. From the moment that he bought his first home on South Prairie Avenue in Chicago and moved her there, he worked to make her life comfortable, even luxurious. The house was not large, but it was furnished with Chinese rugs, a seven-foot bathtub, marble sinks, and full-length mirrors in the den. Teresa had her own apartment of rooms, and delighted in cooking for her children, going to mass at a nearby church, and exchanging recipes with other women in the neighborhood.

Capone tried to ensure his sister's happiness as well. He paid for her to attend a private girls' school in Chicago. During the years that she attended the school, he played Santa Claus every Christmas. His Cadillac would pull up to the door of the

Conservative Capone

In an era when Americans prided themselves on being liberal and open-minded, many of Capone's views on society were surprisingly conservative. Robert Schoenberg details some of the gangster's opinions in Mr. Capone: The Real—And Complete—Story of Al Capone.

Few of Capone's ... pronouncements on society would have ruffled the most stolid burgher [middle-class businessman]. "People respect nothing nowadays," he'd complain. "Once we put virtue, honor, truth, and the law on a pedestal. Our children were brought up to respect things." But now, "look what a mess we've made of life!" He deplored birth control, which sapped America's vitality. He loathed homosexuals. He execrated [hated] the flapper's bobbed hair, showcase clothing and brashness. "The trouble with women today," he'd pontificate, "is their excitement over too many things outside the home. A woman's home and her children are her real happiness...." As for the end of tolerated vice, he said "Reform did not end prostitution." It spread it around and made it dangerous. "Now the girls no longer are inspected once a week by health department doctors. Now they are not concentrated down on the Levee [a lawless section of Chicago]. Instead, they are living in the swank apartment houses, associating with the wives and daughters of the best people in town. They simply went underground."

school, and the driver unloaded boxes of candy, turkeys, baskets of fruit, and gifts for every student and teacher.

When Mafalda grew older and prepared to marry John Maritote, brother of gangster Frank Diamond, Capone spared no expense to make the occasion perfect. The wedding took place on December 14, 1930. Mafalda wore ivory satin, and more than three thousand guests attended the ceremony at St. Mary's Church in Cicero.

After the wedding, the guests moved to the Cotton Club of Cicero, and the bridal couple cut a nine-foot-long wedding cake shaped like an ocean liner. The word *Honolulu* was written on it in red, indicating the couple's honeymoon destination. The cake alone cost Capone more than two thousand dollars. He also bestowed upon the couple fifty thousand dollars and a house as a wedding present.

"Two Gun" Hart

Capone's provision for his family extended to his brothers. Through the organization he supported most of them. The reunion with his oldest brother James was particularly memorable, even though James had chosen a line of work that ran in direct opposition to that of the rest of the family.

When James left home at the age of sixteen, he traveled throughout the Midwest and changed his name to Richard Hart. For a time he worked for a traveling circus. Later, he claimed to

Richard Hart, Capone's oldest brother.

have served in World War I, although he could not produce proof of his war service. He was fascinated with guns and became a crack shot, but instead of breaking the law, he chose to enforce it.

Hart eventually settled in the tiny town of Homer, Nebraska. There he married and became a Prohibition officer. While Al Capone made a name for himself in the bootlegging business, Hart—nicknamed "Two Gun" Hart—raided stills, chased horse thieves, and kept the peace. In 1927, he was one of several bodyguards for Calvin Coolidge when the president took a summer vacation in South Dakota.

Hart reunited with his family in 1924, when the name Al Capone was beginning to make headlines. The lawman and the gangster discovered they had some traits in common. Both were married and had sons. Both were attracted to violence and gunplay. Both took the law into their own hands when it suited their purpose. Hart, in fact, had been involved in the questionable death of a man in 1923.

When the Great Depression brought economic collapse, unemployment, and poverty to America in the 1930s, Hart was hard hit and turned to his brothers for monetary help. With the money he received, he was able to feed his family and keep his home. Hart was grateful to Al and Ralph for their generosity, but he was never comfortable with the fact that they were outlaws. As one historian points out, "For him, the law was the law, and he liked enforcing it."[60]

"All I Get Is Abuse"

Capone resented the fact that Richard Hart and others disapproved of his illegal activities and thought of him as a cold-blooded killer. "I'm known all over the world as a millionaire gorilla," he complained. Rather than a gorilla, he preferred to think of himself as a public benefactor. "I've given people

the light pleasures [liquor and gambling], shown them a good time. And all I get is abuse,"[61] he complained. He was even able to justify his reasons for committing murder. "Maybe [I think] that the law of self-defense, the way God looks at it, is a little broader than the law books have it. . . . Maybe it means killing a man who'd kill you if he saw you first. Maybe it means killing a man in defense of your business. . . . I think it does."[62]

Capone was undoubtedly a killer, and he did hurt many people including ordinary, hardworking citizens who paid too much for the liquor he sold. But he had commendable characteristics, too. He was a patron of the arts and could speak knowledgeably about the theater, movies, jazz, and Italian opera. "Al loved music," a friend recalled. "He bought a phonograph, and he bought every [opera singer Enrico] Caruso record he could find. . . . . He would play them by the hour."[63]

His loyalty was also well known. Men like John Torrio did not have to worry that Capone would betray them. He was always there if needed. His word of honor, if he gave it, was good. In one case, Capone was planning to fix a professional boxing match so that former heavyweight champion Jack Dempsey would win over challenger Gene Tunney. Dempsey begged him not to interfere, and Capone agreed to remain uninvolved. He lost money on the fight, but still sent an elaborate floral arrangement to Dempsey and his wife afterward with a card that said, "To the Dempseys in the name of sportsmanship."[64]

Ready and Willing to Help

Capone's gift to the Dempseys was not exceptional—his generosity was legendary. Christmas shopping for his family and friends could cost him more than $100,000. He threw parties that cost $5,000 and spent $1,800 when he put on a banquet. He was also in the habit of giving each of his friends a belt buckle with their initials set in diamonds. Each buckle cost almost $300; and he could place an order for thirty

Men eat at a soup kitchen established by Capone. He was known for his generosity.

at a time. (At the time, a dinner in a restaurant cost about 65 cents.)

Family and friends were not the only ones to benefit from his giving. He liked to carry a thick wad of cash—up to $50,000—which he pulled out whenever the occasion warranted. He might tip waiters and musicians $100. Even panhandlers were sure of a few dollars if they stopped him on the street. And when he learned that a family by the name of Freeman had been injured during a drive-by shooting in which he was the intended victim, he paid their medical expenses, which totaled more than $10,000. One of his men explained, "The Big Fellow never wants bystanders hurt."[65]

Examples of Capone's aid to those in need were unending, especially if they were members of the Italian American community. He gave money to young people who wanted to go to college. He footed the bill for one young woman's wedding. Merchants in Cicero had standing orders to give coal, groceries, and clothes to the needy, at Capone's expense. One Thanksgiving, Capone gave five thousand turkeys to families who would not otherwise have been able to afford them. During the Great Depression in the 1930s, he established soup kitchens in Chicago that fed three thousand people a day. "You can say what you like about Al Capone," one woman said. "If people were desperate and needed help, he was there to help

them. As long as you were on the up-and-up. He didn't expect anything in return and he never expected you to pay him back."[66]

Capone's readiness to help those in need was not limited to monetary gifts. He was also willing to use his powerful reputation to aid others. One man who knew him explained: "Say that you and your wife had a daughter whose husband was giving her a bad time. Al was the one you'd get to help straighten out the problem."[67] When vaudeville entertainer Harry Richman learned that Capone was a fan and attended many of his shows, he asked the gangster to deal with hoodlums who were robbing him at knifepoint after he left the theater every evening. Capone gave him a note that read, "Anybody who harms Mr. Richman in any way, shape, or form will have to account to me. Yours truly, A. Capone."[68] The next time Richman was held up, the hoodlums read the note, hastily apologized, and left him alone.

Capone and the Younger Generation

Capone was particularly kind when it came to children. As he drove through the residential streets of Chicago, he would sometimes throw silver dollars to small boys who watched him pass. He bought tickets for Boy Scout troops so they could attend baseball games. When he saw a young newsboy out late on a rainy evening, he gave him twenty dollars for all his papers. "Throw them on the floor, [and] run home to your mother,"[69] he directed.

Every child he met found him to be generous and tolerant. During his summer in Lansing, Michigan, Capone often took a group of children to town and bought them new clothes, bicycles, and ice cream. When he played cards with family friends, he enjoyed children being in the room. One young boy remembered, "[My sister] Grazia would crawl under the table and untie everyone's shoes, and the men [playing cards] would pretend not to notice."[70]

Even when it came to daily routines, Capone proved to be thoughtful and tender. When visitors came to the Capone house when Sonny was young, the gangster took time from conversation or meetings to tuck his son in bed at night. One of Capone's critics, pho-

Holding Fast

In his interview with Cornelius Vanderbilt Jr., published in Liberty *magazine on October 17, 1931, Capone talked about the social and economic strains America was feeling as a result of the Great Depression of the 1930s. Capone's concerns focused on ordinary men and women, many of whom he fed in his soup kitchens in Chicago. Vanderbilt's interview with Capone is included in* The Norton Book of Interviews, *edited by Christopher Silvester.*

This is going to be a terrible winter.... Us fellas has gotta open our pocketbooks, and keep on keeping them open, if we want any of us to survive. We can't wait for Congress or Mr. Hoover or anyone else. We must help keep tummies filled and bodies warm.

If we don't, it's all up with the way we've learned to live. Why, do you know, sir, America is on the verge of its greatest social upheaval? Bolshevism [Communism] is knocking at our gates. We can't afford to let it in. We've got to organize ourselves against it, and put our shoulders together and hold fast. We need funds to fight famine....

We must keep America whole, and safe, and unspoiled. If machines are going to take jobs away from the worker, then he will need to find something else to do. Perhaps he'll get back to the soil. But we must care for him during the period of change. We must keep him away from red [communist] literature, red ruses [deceptions]; we must see that his mind remains healthy. For, regardless of where he was born, he is now an American.

A 1930 picture of a bathrobe-clad Capone relaxing with a cigar at his Miami, Florida, home. Capone dreamed of retiring from his gangster lifestyle.

tographer Tony Berardi, stated, "Much as I didn't like the guy, I have to admit he was good with children."[71]

A New Threat

Unfortunately, Capone's good qualities were heavily overshadowed by the criminal life he chose to lead. Repeatedly throughout his life he con-

sidered retiring from bootlegging and racketeering. He dreamed of living a peaceful life on his estate in Florida, and as time passed, he spent more and more time there, fishing, swimming, and running his business affairs long-distance. "I am here for a rest which I think I deserve," he stated to reporters in 1930. "All I wish is to be left alone

and enjoy the home which I have purchased here."[72]

Capone was not destined for peace
and comfort, however. After lengthy
and painstaking efforts, the federal
government had put together enough
incriminating evidence to bring him to
trial. Capone shrugged off this threat
to his future, but he did not take into
account the tenacity and determination
of the Internal Revenue Service and
the Judicial Department. "[Al Capone]
and a supporting army of gangsters and
racketeers have taken [captured] the
first three trenches: city, county and
state forces could not stop them," one
journalist wrote. "Now they are facing
the fourth trench—our national government."[73] In this battle, Capone had
met his match, a foe he could not out-
smart or buy off no matter how hard
he tried.

Chapter Five

"GET CAPONE"

As Al Capone approached his thirtieth birthday, he realized that there was a high price to be paid for living a life of crime. He always had to be on the lookout for police who might carry out unexpected raids or catch him in some illegal act. He was also constantly afraid of being killed by rival gang lords or by hoodlums who wanted to make a name for themselves.

The risk of the latter was so great that at one point he decided he needed life insurance as protection for his family. He checked with six different insurance firms, all of whom refused to insure him because of his extremely hazardous lifestyle. The refusal irked him, but the setback soon became insignificant as the U.S. government's net of investigation began to tighten around him.

Manipulating the Law

In Capone's view, the law had always been a manageable problem, something he could manipulate or evade as it suited his needs. He had personally killed several men, had ordered many more eliminated, had engaged in prostitution and illegal gambling, violated Prohibition, and bribed thousands of police officers and public figures. He had been arrested numerous times for such activities, but only once had he actually spent time behind bars. In 1929 in Philadelphia, after being found guilty of carrying a concealed weapon, he was sentenced to a year in prison in Pennsylvania. When details of the arrest became known, however, some people believed that he had wanted to be locked away for a time. They guessed that his involvement in the St. Valentine's Day massacre had put him in extreme danger from Bugs Moran, or from other gangsters who had experienced reprisals after the event. Prison was a safe place, where he could live until the danger on the outside lessened.

Of course, there had been several unpleasant and embarrassing incidents with the law over the years, but Capone tried to forget them. In 1927, for example, he had made a cross-country railroad trip to California. On his arrival in Los Angeles, he was met by hostility and public protest, and was promptly told to leave town. "You're not wanted here. We're giving you twelve hours to leave,"[74] the chief of police said.

Later that year, he met similar hostility when he, Mae, and Sonny visited Miami, Florida, and tried to buy a home there. Defying the criticism, Capone made his purchase through a third party, then kept a low profile until some of the furor died down. "A little clique . . . has tried to run me out of town, but I refused to be chased,"[75] he told a journalist.

Capone's mug shot from his 1929 arrest for carrying a concealed weapon.

Public Enemy

Shortly after he was freed from prison in Pennsylvania in 1930, Capone was faced with a situation that went beyond embarrassing. In March of that year, Frank Loesch and the Chicago Crime Commission published a Public Enemies list featuring the names of twenty-eight high-ranking Chicago criminals. These included Bugs Moran, Jack

Guzik, Jack McGurn, and Ralph Capone among others. Al Capone was first on the list. Loesch explained, "The purpose is to keep the light of publicity shining on Chicago's most prominent, well-known, and notorious gangsters to the end that they may be under constant observation by the law enforcing authorities and law-abiding citizens."[76]

The distinction of being Public Enemy Number One enraged Capone, who wanted more than anything to be seen as a legitimate, contributing member of society. "I get blamed for everything that goes on here, but I had nothing to do with any of the things you talk about,"[77] he complained to one authority shortly thereafter.

About the same time that Capone was labeled Public Enemy Number One, Ralph Capone was indicted on charges of tax evasion. The FBI had been trying to find evidence that could be used to bring the Capones to justice, and the 1927 Sullivan decision—a ruling by the Supreme Court—made their job easier. The decree meant that beginning in 1927, criminals had to pay taxes on illegal income. Not surprisingly, few did, and the Capones were no exception. In 1926, however, Ralph had foolishly declared income in the amount of fifty-five thousand dollars for the previous four years. When the government discovered that he had failed to pay taxes on that amount, and also had substantial bank accounts under several fictitious names which might also be tax-

able, they believed they had the evidence they needed to prosecute.

Ralph's trial in federal court began in April 1930, and once the facts were presented, it took a jury less than three hours to convict him of tax evasion. He was sentenced to three years in a federal penitentiary and ordered to pay a fine of up to forty thousand dollars.

After Ralph's conviction, Al Capone realized that the government was serious in its pursuit of him as well. He was right. In March 1929, Herbert Hoover became president of the United States. In his first months in office, he learned about Al Capone's crime empire and the gangster's ability to evade the legal consequences of his misdeeds. Hoover decided it was time for the gang lord's reign to end. "Have you got that fellow Capone, yet?" he would demand of his advisers regularly. "Remember, now; I want that man Capone in jail."[78]

The Untouchables

At Hoover's insistence, the federal government set out to "get Capone" in two different ways. The first was a concentrated effort to shut down his illegal liquor business and gain hard evidence of his Prohibition violations. Heading that effort was a young Treasury agent named Eliot Ness, who went after the gangster with unswerving dedication and single-mindedness.

Ness was born on April 19, 1903, in Chicago. He grew up in a well-to-do environment and graduated from the

September 1929, and he quickly selected a small team of trustworthy men to assist him. He later described how he had chosen them:

I ticked off the general qualities I desired: single, no older than thirty, both the mental and physical stamina to work long hours and the courage and ability to use fist or gun and special investigative techniques. I needed a good telephone man, one who could tap a wire with speed and precision. I needed men who were excellent drivers, for much of our success would depend upon how expertly they could trail the mob's cars and trucks . . . and fresh faces—from other divisions—who were not known to the Chicago mobsters.[79]

FBI agent Eliot Ness was assigned to break up Capone's illegal liquor operations.

University of Chicago in 1925 in the top third of his class. Although Ness's family was willing to support him through law school, Ness was attracted to the field of law enforcement instead. His brother-in-law was an FBI agent who taught him marksmanship and also recommended him for a position on the Prohibition Bureau.

Ness was officially assigned to break up Capone's liquor operations in

At a time when Prohibition agents were notorious for taking bribes and payoffs, Ness and his men were soon nicknamed the "Untouchables" because of their honesty and integrity. Over the next months, they raided countless Capone breweries and speakeasies. They relied on surprise and a ten-ton flatbed truck, outfitted with ladders for scaling walls and a reinforced steel bumper to smash down doors. In the course of a few months, they successfully closed down operations worth up to $1 million to Capone.

Capone first met such assaults on his business in the usual way. He tried to bribe Ness to stop, offering him $2,000 a week as payoff. Ness was only making $2,500 a year as a federal agent, but he refused the money. Later, Ness called a press conference and explained. "Possibly it wasn't too important for the world to know that we couldn't be bought, but I did want Al Capone and every gangster in the city to realize that there were still a few law enforcement agents who couldn't be swerved from their duty."[80]

Unable to bribe Ness, Capone turned to violence. On several occasions, his men tried to kill the young Prohibition agent, and they did murder one of Ness's assistants. Ness boldly showed his defiance by staging a parade of trucks he had captured from Capone. He directed that they be driven down the street past Capone's headquarters. Ness then called Capone and taunted him over the phone. "If you look out your front windows down onto Michigan Avenue at exactly eleven o'clock you'll see something that should interest you."[81] When Capone realized what was happening, he was infuriated and reportedly stormed away

Opposites

Beginning in 1929, Prohibition agent Eliot Ness was unswerving in his determination to rid Chicago of Al Capone's bootleg empire. The contrast between the two archenemies was striking, as Laurence Bergreen describes in Capone: The Man and His Era.

In many ways, [Eliot Ness served] as a remarkable foil [contrast] to Al Capone. The gangster controlled a national crime network generating $75 million a year; the honest young Prohibition agent's annual salary came to just $2,500. Capone was often flamboyant and vicious; Ness was boyish, vague, hard to read. Capone was fat and dark; Ness stood six feet tall, and he was rather gangly, with sleepy blue eyes. Capone's shiny custom-made suits shouted "gangster"; Ness dressed conservatively and parted his cornsilk hair in the middle. Capone's gray eyes and dark hair, not to mention his double scar, gave him an aura of implacable [relentless] menace; Ness, in contrast, was genuinely handsome, [actor] Gary Cooper handsome. Capone raged against his enemies and even took a baseball bat to three of his victims; Ness never lost his temper and always contained his emotions.

from the windows, yelling obscenities and breaking the furniture.

"Hanging a Foreclosure Sign on the Moon"

Despite Capone's attempts, the Untouchables survived and continued their antibootlegging efforts. Not only were they key players in bringing Capone down, but they also served an

Frank J. Wilson led the investigation into Capone's income tax evasion.

equally important function by distracting the gangster from the federal government's other approach—a tax investigation—to bring him to justice.

As early as 1927, Elmer Irey, head of the Special Intelligence Unit of the Internal Revenue Service, had begun the task of proving that Capone had failed to pay income tax on money he made. In 1928, Irey assigned one of his most relentless investigators, Frank J. Wilson, to search for evidence that would show that Capone had income in excess of five thousand dollars annually, the standard exemption at the time.

The task was extremely difficult. Unlike Ralph, Al Capone and his bookkeepers had been extremely wily. Wilson noted "[Al Capone] was completely anonymous when it came to income. He did all his business through front men or third parties."[82] His expensive home in Florida was in Mae's name. Most of his income from prostitution and gambling came in the form of cash. He had not endorsed a check for years, had no bank accounts in his own name, and left accounting of his businesses to Jack Guzik. A colleague of Wilson's warned him that convicting Capone for tax evasion "would

The Sullivan Decision

Law enforcement found it impossible to convict Capone of murder, racketeering, and bootlegging, but the Internal Revenue Service believed it could bring him to justice on tax evasion charges. Their efforts were aided by the Sullivan decision, which took effect in 1927. Biographer John Kobler gives details of the Sullivan decision and its effects in Capone: The Life and World of Al Capone.

As early as 1927, Elmer L. Irey, the chief of Internal Revenue's Enforcement Branch, was given a powerful weapon to wield against gangsters. That year the Supreme Court handed down its decision in the case on appeal of a bootlegger named Manley Sullivan, who had filed no tax return on the grounds that income from illegal transactions was not taxable, and moreover, that to declare such income would be self-incriminatory within the meaning of the Fifth Amendment [no person shall be required to testify against himself in a criminal case]. The Supreme Court ruled against him, finding no reason "why the fact that a business is unlawful should exempt it from paying taxes that if lawful it would have to pay." As for self-incrimination, "It would be an extreme if not extravagant application of the Fifth Amendment to say that it authorized a man to refuse to state the amount of his income because it had been made in crime."

be as easy as hanging a foreclosure sign on the moon."[83]

Persistence and Ingenuity

Wilson was not discouraged. He went to work, careful to remain as inconspicuous as possible. Fortunately, he looked like an ordinary businessman, balding, bespectacled, and dressed in a wrinkled suit, and thus did not draw attention to himself through his appearance. He stayed for short periods of time in drab rooming houses. He placed all his calls from public telephones. He also sneaked two undercover agents into Capone's organization.

Both of these men proved invaluable. Not only did they gain inside details about Capone's comings and goings, but one learned in the nick of time that Wilson had somehow been noticed by Capone and was targeted for assassination. Despite instructions never to make direct contact with his boss, the agent called Wilson at his hotel and said, "The big fellow is going to get you. . . . You've got to get out of there, Frank. Get out this afternoon."[84]

Wilson obeyed, but vowed to get Capone if he accomplished nothing else in his career.

Wilson's second agent uncovered information that proved to be equally important. He reported that a Capone employee had made a comment about a raid on the Hawthorne Smoke Shop, one of Capone's gambling dens, which had taken place five years earlier. The employee stated that incriminating evidence against Capone had been taken in that raid, but law enforcement officials had not recognized its importance. "They walked out with a nice book of figures from the smoke shop that they could've used against the Big Boy only they overlooked it,"[85] the employee said.

Wilson realized that he had damaging information on Capone in his possessions—he just had to find it. Energized, he searched until he found an overlooked ledger that contained headings reading "21," "Faro," "Roulette," and "Horse bets." It showed income for the many illegal activities the Capone organization operated.

Wilson still had to connect this income directly to Capone, however. To do that, he tracked down two of Capone's former employees and convinced them to talk. One was cashier Fred Ries, who reportedly had inside information on payments made to Capone. The other was Leslie Shumway, a bookkeeper for the Capone organization. Both initially refused to cooperate, but after much persuasion and promises of protection, Wilson got the information he needed.

"A Man of Unbelievable Arrogance"

On June 5, 1931, a grand jury returned an indictment against Al Capone for twenty-two counts of tax evasion on revenue totaling more than $1 million. The figure did not cover the whole of Capone's multimillion-dollar income, but it was enough for the government's purposes. A week later, a second grand jury indicted the gangster for more than five thousand violations of the Volstead Act, the legislation that formally made Prohibition a law. Because the income tax violations were more serious, however, they took priority over the liquor infringements.

Capone's trial was set for June 16, 1931, in Chicago. James H. Wilkerson, a short, bushy-browed judge with a testy, no-nonsense style, had been assigned to preside over the case. Capone's attorneys were Michael Ahearn and Albert Fink, and U.S. attorney George E.Q. Johnson represented the government. Johnson, a tall, wiry man who wore tweed suits and parted his unruly hair in the middle, described Capone as a "man of unbelievable arrogance,"[86] and was determined to bring him to justice.

Capone arrived at the Federal Building, where the trial was to take place, wearing a banana yellow suit and

Capone, seated next to his lawyers at the 1931 hearings of the federal grand jury, is indicted for income tax evasion.

a beaming smile. Assured by his lawyers that they had arranged for him to cut a deal and avoid serious penalties, he pleaded guilty on all counts. Wilkerson then set the sentencing date for June 30, and everyone left the court.

On June 30, however, events did not go as planned. In the days preceding the hearing, the newspapers had predicted that Capone would receive only a two-and-a-half-year sentence. The gangster himself had brazenly boasted of it. Judge Wilkerson was irate. When court convened, he stated:

There have been some publications which were contemptuous in character, and tending to bring the administration of justice in the federal court into disrepute. They have even gone too far as to announce in advance what the period of punishment would be. It is time for somebody to impress upon this defendant that it is utterly impossible to bargain with a federal court.[87]

Realizing that their client might face serious consequences if he continued to plead guilty, the defense team went into conference. In the end, they advised Capone to change his plea to not guilty. The trial was once again rescheduled, this time to October. When asked what he thought about his chances of winning, Capone replied, "I believe I've got at least an even break."[88]

The Case Goes to Court

Capone was not content with an even break, however. He preferred tilting the odds in his favor. A few days before the trial got under way, Frank Wilson learned that the gangster had obtained the names of the men who had been called to serve on his jury. Capone's henchmen were bribing and threatening the jurists to influence their decision.

Wilson took the information to Judge Wilkerson, who remained surprisingly calm. "Bring your case into court as planned, gentlemen. Leave the rest to me,"[89] he said reassuringly. Next morning, when Capone and his lawyers seated themselves in front of him, Wilkerson abruptly traded his jurists for twelve men who had been chosen for a trial in another courtroom.

Such complications were only the beginning of the drama and excitement that surrounded Capone's days in court. One day, proceedings halted while Capone's bodyguard, Philip D'Andrea, was hustled out of court because he was wearing a gun; D'Andrea was later found guilty of contempt for carrying a concealed weapon. Another time, film star Edward G. Robinson, who starred in many gangster roles inspired by Capone's life story, caused a sensation when he appeared to watch the proceedings.

Despite the distractions, Johnson proceeded to make the case against Capone. He called a variety of witnesses who testified to the generous gifts the gangster gave his friends, to the large amounts of money he spent on his clothes, and to the magnificence of his home. Johnson made the point that Capone had come from a poor family, and had never inherited money. Yet he always had plenty to spend. That money, Johnson contended, had to be money he made, either legally or illegally.

When it came to a defense, Capone's attorneys mounted a weak case. They emphasized that their client had no income of record, then called a series of bookies and gamblers who claimed that Capone's money came from gambling wins. Because he was a poor gambler, however, they said, he had lost most of it. Everyone on the jury knew the unspoken truth, however—the gangster

Wait and See

When Cornelius Vanderbilt Jr. interviewed Al Capone for Liberty *magazine in 1931, Capone spoke about the early days of his tax evasion trial and the unsuccessful efforts of his lawyers to plea bargain. His cocky remarks undoubtedly masked the concern he must have felt for his life and his future. The Vanderbilt interview is included in* The Norton Book of Interviews, *edited by Christopher Silvester.*

When I was held the other day for evasion of federal taxes I nearly got myself into a fine pickle. Certain officials wished to make a bargain with me. If I'd plead guilty and go to jail for two and a half years they'd dismiss the charges they had against me. A pretty penny had to be paid, but I thought that that was better than the strain of a long-winded trial. A day or so before the bargain was to be struck, though, I learned that someone was going to go to the Appellate Court and that there'd be a fly in the ointment and they'd have me in Leavenworth [penitentiary] for ten and a half years. So I decided I could be just as foxy [tricky], and we entered a plea of not guilty, and when the case comes up we'll see what we will see.

raked in millions annually from his criminal enterprises.

Johnson's final summation on October 17 emphasized his scorn of the defense's arguments. "What a picture we have in this case: no income, but diamond belt buckles, twenty-seven dollar shirts, furnishings for his home—$116,000 that is not deductible from his income. And yet counsel comes here and argues to you that the man has no income!"[90]

"A Smashing Blow"

On the evening of October 17, the jury returned a verdict. Despite the mountain of circumstantial evidence against

Capone, they found him guilty on only five of the twenty-two counts—three felonies for evading taxes and two misdemeanors for failing to file income tax returns.

Capone accepted the verdict stoically. He assumed that, as in previous cases, he would have to pay a fine and perhaps serve a year or two behind bars. Judge Wilkerson was not about to let him off so easily, however. On October 24, he sentenced Capone to eleven years in prison and fined him fifty thousand plus court costs. Capone was also required to pay a tax bill of more than one hundred thousand. His jail sentence was to begin immediately. "It was a smashing blow to

Capone is escorted from Chicago Federal Court after being sentenced to eleven years in prison for tax evasion.

the massive gang chief," wrote one journalist. "He tried to take it with a smile, but that smile was almost pitiful. His clumsy fingers, tightly locked behind his back, twitched and twisted."[91]

As Capone left the courtroom, reporters asked him what he thought of the sentence. "It was a little below the belt, but I guess if I have to do it I can,"[92] he replied.

He had no intention of suffering more than was necessary, however. While his lawyers appealed, he was taken to Cook County jail, where he soon bribed the warden into giving him a one-man cell with a private shower. He also was allowed to make phone calls, send telegrams, and, in effect, conduct business from behind bars. The situation continued until the Department of Justice learned of the special considerations. After that, his privileges were cut off, and visits from outsiders were curtailed.

On May 2, 1932, Capone's appeal to a higher court was denied. Authorities set in motion plans to transfer him to federal facilities. On May 4, he arrived at Atlanta Penitentiary in Georgia, a tough, overcrowded stone facility headed by Warden A.C. Aderhold. "Good-bye, Al. . . . Good luck, Al. . . . You got a bum break, Al,"[93] his fellow inmates called as he set off from Cook County.

"I'll bet Mussolini never got a send-off like this,"[94] Capone quipped. It was an arrogant remark, characteristic of the gangster. His past experiences led him to believe that he would be able to manipulate the system, bribe prison authorities to get special privileges, perhaps even continue to run his crime empire from prison. It would not be long before he realized that all that was in the past. The future would be as painful and demeaning as any punishment he had ever dealt out to his enemies.

Chapter Six

PRISONER NUMBER 85

Upon his arrival in Atlanta in 1932, Capone discovered that this prison did not allow many opportunities for soliciting special favors. He was treated like any other new inmate—given a haircut, a set of blue denim overalls, and a cell mate. Like everyone else, he was expected to follow prison routine. Guards were aloof and businesslike. Warden Aderhold was an incorruptible man who had no intention of allowing the crime kingpin any more privileges than anyone else.

Life looked bleak, but there was nothing for Capone to do but settle into his new routine and try to stop thinking about the life he had left behind. Just when that seemed manageable, a heavier blow fell. Atlanta would not be the worst punishment he would have to endure.

"A Hulking Figure"

Capone found the narrow and boring routine at Atlanta maddening. The days were long, punctuated by meals and head counts conducted by the guards. All inmates worked; Capone was assigned a job in the shoe factory. A reporter who visited the penitentiary described him there. "A hulking figure in cheap, baggy cotton clothing, swart-skinned, sits hunched over a whirling electric stitching machine. Hands once soft from a life of luxurious ease . . . now calloused, deftly fit a heavy strip of sole leather on a bulky, shapeless shoe upper. . . . The machine thumps and pounds."[95]

After a while, Capone welcomed the distraction that work provided. He had difficulty sleeping at night, and his free time (a few minutes each day and on the weekends) was often stressful. The prison was crowded with bootleggers, murderers, and other serious offenders who taunted and harassed him for being brought down by the government. Some picked fights; others started rumors, which soon spread

Capone plays cards on the train ride to Atlanta where he began serving his prison term in 1932.

outside the prison, that Capone enjoyed special privileges. One claimed he smoked two-dollar cigars. Others claimed he wore special shoes, that he had extra sets of underwear, and that he kept a stash of money, used for bribing guards, hidden away in a hollowed-out broom handle.

When word leaked out, the warden denied all such accusations, claiming that Capone was more strictly monitored than any other prisoner. The FBI checked out the situation, and found no evidence of favoritism either. Nevertheless, rumors persisted, reaching as high as the House of Representatives and other U.S. government officials.

Island of the Pelicans

Attorney General Homer S. Cummings was one of the officials to hear the rumors. A man of action who had the power to accomplish what others could not, he had already thought of creating a tough new prison to house criminals like Capone. In May 1934, he announced the imminent opening of that new prison. In the words of one historian, "[The facility would] demonstrate to all Americans—especially gangsters—that the U.S. government would not tolerate lawlessness and violence."[96]

Cummings had said he wanted the new prison to be in an isolated spot from which prisoners could not escape, "a remote place—on an island or in

Alaska, so that the persons incarcerated would not be in constant communication with friends outside."[97] In August of 1933, the Justice Department chose a site—Alcatraz Island, which early Spanish explorers called "Island of the Pelicans"—located in San Francisco Bay, one and a quarter miles off the mainland.

A more escape-proof locale would have been hard to find. Alcatraz was a former military prison perched atop stark, windswept cliffs. Strong currents, icy water, and sharks in the bay made swimming to land virtually impossible. The Justice Department spent more than a quarter of a million dollars to strengthen security, add gun galleries and watchtowers, and install sensitive metal detectors and even electronically-controlled steel panels to guard locks.

The man placed in charge of the facility, Warden James A. Johnston, was committed to maintaining the strictest discipline. Life at Alcatraz

The island prison of Alcatraz. Capone was among the first to serve a prison sentence here.

would be totally supervised, violations of the rules severely punished, and communication with outsiders almost nonexistent. Johnston stated, "They [the prisoners] are not even going to have an opportunity to know what goes on outside. Those men were sent here because the government wants to break their contacts with the underworld. That is going to be done."[98]

The Rock

Word of the new prison—nicknamed "The Rock"—soon made its way through the inmate population at Atlanta. Rumors went around that no one ever came back from Alcatraz, that going there was the equivalent of a death sentence. Even the most hardened prisoners were afraid.

When Capone learned in August 1934 that he was slated to be one of the first transferees, he lost control. His cell mate Red Rudensky remembered that he saw "all the fire and hate and strength and torment erupt suddenly. He was all power and anger as he leaped at the nearest guard, shouting obscenities."[99]

Resistance was fruitless, however. At midnight on August 19, Capone and several other prisoners were shackled and taken in great secrecy to a train bound for the West Coast. Authorities feared that associates on the outside might try to hijack the train and stage an escape, so windows were barred and guards stood at the ready throughout the entire trip.

When the train arrived in the San Francisco Bay area, the railroad cars holding the prisoners were transferred to a ferry and transported across the water. Only then were they opened, and the men marched up a steep slope to the cell house atop the hill. There, the warden met them, and Johnston got his first look at Capone. He later recalled:

Before I called him to the desk for instructions I could see him nudging the prisoners near him and slipping them some corner-of-the-mouth comment. . . . It was apparent he wanted to impress other prisoners by asking me questions as if he were their leader. I wanted to make sure they didn't get any such idea. I handed him a ticket with his number, 85, gave him the instructions I had given to every other man, and told him to move along.[100]

"The Wop with the Mop"

If Capone had had visions of himself as a captain of men, it soon became clear that there was little chance for leadership, or even friendship, among the inmates on the Island of the Pelicans. Each man spent most of his time alone in a nine-by-five-foot cell equipped with a drop-down cot, table, chair, washstand, and toilet. The most ordinary aspects of daily

The Lindbergh Kidnapping

Capone was behind bars when aviator Charles Lindbergh's infant son was kidnapped on March 1, 1932, but the gangster was horrified by the act and offered to help. He claimed that with his contacts in the underworld, he might be able to secure the child's release when others could not. As Robert Schoenberg describes in Mr. Capone: The Real—And Complete—Story of Al Capone, *law enforcement officials had no intention of letting Capone get involved.*

If the government would let Capone out temporarily, Capone thought he could effect the baby's return within forty-eight hours. "I know a lot of people who might be valuable in finding the child," Capone's message ran. "There's nothing I can do here behind the bars, but I'm pretty sure there would be if I could get out for a while." He explained to Hearst [newspaper] editor Arthur Brisbane that he didn't expect freedom, just ad hoc [unofficial] parole. . . . He told the editor that he'd "give any bond they require," and leave his brother, John, as hostage against his return to jail. "You don't suppose I would doublecross my own brother?" he asked. . . .

After Capone's offer, the Lindberghs called in SIU [Special Intelligence Unit] agents Arthur Madden and Frank Wilson, who presumably knew how to deal with him. On their advice, the family turned down the offer. Capone renewed it six weeks later, after the distraught parents paid $50,000 ransom yet did not get back their son (who in fact had been murdered). Although they would give "credit where it's due" if Capone got their baby back, the Lindberghs still refused to call for Capone's release. After working so long and hard to get him, the government probably would not have let him go anyway.

routine were supervised. For instance, inmates were allowed to shave three times a week in their cell. A razor blade was passed through the bars and then reclaimed three minutes later by the guard.

Three daily mealtimes in the prison cafeteria were short and marked by total silence. Food was well prepared and plentiful. One typical dinner included soup, casserole, beans, cabbage, onions, chili peppers, biscuits, pudding, ice cream, tea, and coffee. Inmates were required to eat, and if they refused three meals in a row, they were placed in isolation. Since inmates were also issued knives, forks, and spoons, they were closely watched during meals, and had to pass through metal detectors before returning to their cells. Everyone also knew that canisters of tear gas were installed in the cafeteria ceiling, to be released the moment anyone became disorderly. Because of that, the room was quickly nicknamed "the Gas Chamber."

As in Atlanta, all inmates had jobs, but in Alcatraz, they worked all day in silence, with only two breaks during which they could talk and smoke. (Cigarettes were a permissible luxury.

A view of one of the long, three-storied corridors inside a cell block at Alcatraz.

Men were issued three packs a week, and each cell block had dispensers of tobacco and papers so inmates could roll their own.) At first, Capone was assigned to work in the laundry. Later he was reassigned to scrub floors in the bathhouse, earning the nickname "the wop [Italian] with the mop."[101]

"Fun" on the Rock

Pleasure was almost unheard of in Alcatraz. The few diversions that were allowed included a Saturday morning bath and two hours to talk, exercise, and work at a chosen hobby on the weekend. Capone, who loved music, learned to play the banjo and a lutelike instrument called a mandola. When he offered to pay to set up a prison band, however, Warden Johnston refused. He was afraid that Capone would demand favors from those who used his instruments. After a time, Johnston relented and allowed interested inmates to form a band if they paid for their own instruments.

Men could visit the prison library, but reading material was heavily censored. Mail was censored as well, and inmates could send only one letter a week to immediate family members. Visits from outsiders had to be approved, were limited to two persons at a time, and could last only twenty minutes. During the visit, both sides peered through a three-by-nine-inch glass-covered hole in a wall and talked through a screened panel. Acoustics were so bad that conversations had to be shouted. The setup was purposefully designed to discourage the discussion of personal or forbidden topics.

Aside from such simple pleasures, there were no special privileges or incentives for good behavior in Alcatraz. Even the mildest infractions were punished, and almost every man earned time in isolation—locked in a bare cell in total darkness, fed with bread and water slipped through a slot in the door. Capone first experienced isolation in late 1934, after he and another inmate got into a fight in the laundry. His punishment lasted only one night, but other men were locked up for weeks at a time. Some lost their minds as a result of the darkness and deprivation they experienced. Others committed suicide.

Hard Times

Fear was a daily part of life in Alcatraz. The prison was filled with the nation's most desperate criminals, angry at being incarcerated and looking for trouble. With plenty of time to think and plan, they were able to create crude weapons, outwit the guards, carry out swift attacks on each other, even make escape plans. During Capone's term, five men tried to escape, although none were successful.

As had been the case in Atlanta, Capone's reputation as a killer and a public enemy caused many to want to

Pushed to the Brink

The repressive regime in Alcatraz proved tough on even the most hardened criminals, as the following incident, described in Laurence Bergreen's Capone: The Man and His Era, *shows. As time passed, more and more Americans came to believe that prison authorities there went beyond the bounds of humanity in their efforts to control their inmates.*

In April [1936], "Dutch" Bowers, a post office safe cracker, became the first inmate to attempt to escape the Rock. He had previously tried to commit suicide … by breaking his glasses and slashing his throat. Once he recovered, he was assigned to a work detail at the incinerator; one afternoon he started chasing a windblown piece of paper and suddenly broke for the barbed wire surrounding the perimeter of the island. Guards shouted for him to halt, but he ignored them and hauled himself up the wire, across the rocks and across the pounding surf. Two guards fired on him, and he fell fifty feet, breaking his neck. The inmates saw in the foolish escape attempt proof that Bowers had gone "stir bugs" [crazy]. That horrifying death and Capone's stabbing generated further publicity, all of it portraying Alcatraz as a penal colony of men pushed to the brink of sanity, an unimaginable hell located right in San Francisco Bay. A growing sector of the public viewed Alcatraz as an exercise in government-sponsored sadism [torture] rather than the last word in criminal deterrence.

challenge him, to test his toughness. Several times he was physically attacked. For instance, when he refused to take part in a prison strike, one of the strikers threw a solid iron sash weight at him, cutting his arm deeply. (In older homes, sash weights allowed wooden-framed windows to be raised and lowered easily.) Another time, an inmate sneaked a pair of scissors out of the barbershop and stabbed Capone in the back, sending him to the infirmary for a week. "When the shirt was removed they [the doctor and attendants] saw all the stab wounds, including one real bad one near the kidneys,"[102] remembered the inmate who helped Capone to the infirmary.

While some prisoners hated Capone, he had allies as well. "Capone got along as well as most others and better than some,"[103] observed one man. These friends also formed a sort of protective society to help shield him from unexpected assault, especially as the years passed and his physical health deteriorated.

Anti-Capone

Some of Capone's worst enemies on Alcatraz were a group of men known as the Texas Cowboys. Their harassment of Capone is described in Laurence Bergreen's Capone: The Man and His Era.

Capone attracted a new tormentor named Jimmy Lucas, an ornery little (140-pound) hard case, as his prior record demonstrated. Serving a life sentence for murder, he had escaped from Huntsville, Texas, penitentiary; while on the loose, he robbed a bank, was recaptured, and sent to Leavenworth [penitentiary]; and from there he had been transferred to the Rock in January 1935 to serve a thirty-year sentence.... Lucas belonged to an entrenched clique of inmates from Texas and Oklahoma; ... they hated Capone, and they vowed to get him any way they could. The clique, known as the Texas Cowboys, started spreading rumors that Capone was ratting on the other inmates. Was a guard accepting favors from a prisoner? Capone was said to have turned them in. Was an inmate somehow found to have concealed a bottle of whiskey in his cell? Capone had told the guards. There was no truth to the rumors, but their mere existence polarized the inmates into pro- and anti-Capone factions. Al Best, number 107, belonged to the small group who remained loyal to Capone. "Outside of losing his head so easily and bragging about what he had done, Capone has a heart as big as a house," Best wrote after he was freed in 1937. "He wanted to do his time in Alcatraz as easy as he could—but the majority of the men had it in for him and were out to get him."

"Very Unstable"

Like all prisoners, Capone received a physical examination, including vaccinations and blood tests, upon his arrival at the penitentiary at Atlanta. There, prison doctors diagnosed him as having tertiary syphilis, a rare, advanced form of the sexually transmitted disease. Although he had experienced no symptoms throughout the years, his early infection had spread to his central nervous system.

In 1933, doctors noted that mild symptoms were starting to appear. They included degeneration of the reflexes, loss of muscular coordination, psychosis, and mental disorientation. Capone also exhibited megalomania—delusions of grandeur—which was another expression of the disease.

Capone's illness produced more symptoms as time passed. The first serious ones appeared in February

1938. One morning, on the way to breakfast, he did not get in line when ordered to do so by the guards. When the warden spoke to him, he appeared disoriented. A short time later, he went into convulsions and had to be taken to the infirmary. There, tests revealed that his condition had worsened, and he was moved from his regular cell block to a cell in the hospital ward where he remained indefinitely.

Although Capone did not realize it, his days as a normally functioning human being had ended. He developed a shuffling walk, a typical sign of neurosyphilis. His speech became slurred. He was unable to concentrate and at times lost touch with reality. Much of the time he muttered and sang to himself, and was content to sit on his bunk and look at a picture of his wife and son. A Federal Bureau of Prisons health report in 1938 noted:

He . . . has some disturbances of consciousness at times as his mind wanders and he hears God and the Angels verbally reply to prayers etc. He however retains partial insight into

these and says that he probably imagines some of the things he hears. . . . He is very unstable and easily aroused by any excitement or confusion taking place on the Ward.[104]

A balding and worn-looking Capone has a mug shot taken for his transfer to a correctional institution on Terminal Island in Los Angeles.

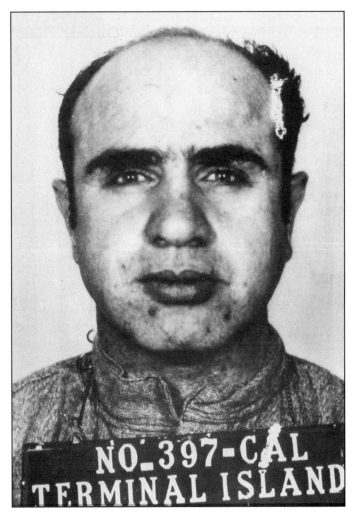

Time to Move On

With almost every passing day, Capone became more childlike. He would brag about his past accomplishments and make up stories about how powerful he had once been. He became difficult to control when something bothered him. And he got involved in name-calling squabbles with other prisoners in the hospital ward.

The crowning incident came when Capone clashed with bank robber Carl Janaway, who had gone "stir-bugs," or insane as a result of long, close confinement. Janaway had been placed in a cell next to Capone. One afternoon, both men became angry at each other. As the insults grew stronger, Janaway began hurling the contents of his bedpan at Capone. Capone retaliated in kind. By the time officials arrived to break up the fight, both men and their cells were covered with excrement.

The situation served to convince prison authorities that Number 85 had become too difficult to manage within the confines of Alcatraz. They decided that the time had come for him to be moved to a place where he could have access to better medical facilities.

On January 6, 1939, after four and a half years in Alcatraz, Capone was escorted under armed guard to the ferry that would take him back to the mainland. He was not yet free to go home, but he was one step closer to the freedom of which he had long dreamed.

Chapter Seven

The Legacy of Capone

The final chapter of Al Capone's life was tragic, as the once-powerful villain degenerated into a confused and simpleminded invalid, disregarded by business associates and forgotten by the public. He lived comfortably on money funneled to him from the organization by his brother Ralph, but because he did not legally own the speakeasies, brothels, and gambling houses that were the sources of his wealth, he left no fortune when he died. One historian writes, "Because of his caution, and his luck, he contrived to escape the doom he knew—sudden death from gunfire—only to fall victim to the doom he at first refused to acknowledge and later failed to comprehend because it had destroyed his mind: slow death from tertiary syphilis."[105]

Release

After leaving Alcatraz, Al Capone was transferred to a hospital at the Federal Correctional Institution on Terminal Island in Los Angeles. In November 1939, Capone's family paid the last of the fines that had been imposed by Judge Wilkerson, and he was moved to the U.S. penitentiary at Lewisburg, Pennsylvania. On November 16, the former crime lord was paroled into the custody of Mae and twenty-year-old Sonny.

Mae Capone immediately sought further medical help for her husband. She took him directly to Baltimore, Maryland, to consult with Johns Hopkins University specialist Dr. Joseph Moore, an expert in neurosyphilis. There were no definitive cures for the disease at the time, but

Moore offered the latest in experimental treatments, the most promising of which was malaria therapy.

Malaria therapy was rooted in the observations of Russian physicians who treated army officers returning from duty in the Caucasus Mountains in Russia. Most of these officers were infected with syphilis. Those who had also had malaria, however, never developed the tertiary form of the disease. Moore had experimented with the therapy before, but not on someone who already had advanced tertiary syphilis. He could only hope that the high fevers common to malaria would kill some or all of Capone's bacteria and improve his condition.

Moore thus injected Capone with malaria parasites, and allowed the

Capone's mother Teresa and brother Ralph are photographed en route to Alcatraz for a visit.

Memories of Capone

Anyone who studies Al Capone's life comes away with innumerable impressions of the man, both good and bad. In Capone: The Man and His Era, *Laurence Bergreen describes the various roles the infamous American filled during the course of his life.*

In his forty-eight years, Capone led many lives, public and private, valiant and contemptible. At various times he was a pimp, a loving husband, a murderer, a bootlegger, martyr, role model, antihero—Public Enemy Number 1. He left behind so many lasting, unexpected impressions. . . . The trustworthy young apprentice to Johnny Torrio; . . . flinging coins from his car as he drove through the streets of Chicago Heights; . . . assenting to "Machine Gun" Jack McGurn's plan for the St. Valentine's Day Massacre; . . . murdering three would-be traitors with a baseball bat; . . . raging at a waiter who dared serve him domestic Parmesan cheese; . . . running a soup kitchen to feed thousands of unemployed men during the Depression; . . . fitting a new suit during his tax trial; . . . journeying through the summer heat to Alcatraz, his legs shackled; . . . hiding under his blanket during a prison riot; . . . rough-housing with his estranged brother's boys. . . .

Acts of grace and mortal sins, one leading inexplicably yet inevitably to another.

resulting episodes of fever to run their course. One observer wrote, "His [Capone's] chills come on every second day and Moore plans to keep him in bed here until he has had fifteen of them."[106] Capone's syphilis was so far advanced, however, that Moore's experimental treatment produced little change in his condition. It was not until 1942, when penicillin became available for treatment of syphilis, that doctors were able to fully eradicate Capone's infection. Even then, however, the antibiotic could not reverse the damaging effects of the disease.

Decline of an Underworld King

After finishing his course of malaria therapy in March 1940, Capone and his family headed south to their home in Miami. Even though the gang lord did not remember the gracious estate on Palm Island, he soon settled into a new, quiet routine there. Protected from the public by the estate's high walls, he could walk about the grounds or hit a tennis ball against a backboard undisturbed. Dressed in pajamas and robe, he passed many hours sitting on his dock in the sun, a fishing pole in his hands. On rare occasions he went out shopping, although never alone.

Capone's son Albert (Sonny) and his bride are pictured here as they leave St. Patrick's Church in Miami after their 1940 wedding.

Capone enjoyed playing gin rummy and pinochle, although he was not capable of making the calculations the game demanded. Knowing it pleased him, his friends and family tried to let him win, and were tolerant of his irritable outbursts when he lost and shouted, "Get the boys. I want this wise guy taken care of."[107]

Capone continued to enjoy his family as well. Sonny married in 1940 and moved to his own home in 1941. He was honest and uninvolved in criminal activities, but still maintained

Unforgettable

The qualities that made Al Capone notorious are some of the same that keep his memory alive today. In Mr. Capone: The Real—And Complete—Story of Al Capone, *Robert Schoenberg explains how the crime lord's villainy and his humanity make him one of America's most famous public enemies of all time.*

Al Capone was, beyond question, the world's best-known gangster, and one of the best-known Americans. His name is still recognized everywhere, without any explanation needed about who he was or what he stands for. . . . The city fathers of Cicero, Illinois, still occasionally ponder the wisdom of changing their town's name to "Hawthorne," its citizens weary of the snide looks and cracks they receive wherever they go because Capone made Cicero his headquarters. . . .

"There are three ways to make a gangster or hoodlum interesting," wrote film critic John Simon. "He can be so brutally and unrestrainedly criminal that he compels our attention; or he can be a master criminal of such cunning and competence he mocks all punishment until some simple, unexpected human flaw betrays him; or he can be, for all his criminality, so human he inspires thoughts of 'There, but for the grace of God. . . .'"

Again and again, Al Capone exemplified, in turn, all three.

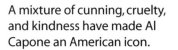
A mixture of cunning, cruelty, and kindness have made Al Capone an American icon.

a close relationship with his parents. He visited them regularly, and nothing pleased Capone more than to purchase gifts for Sonny's daughters.

In 1941, Capone traveled to the family home in Wisconsin to spend time with his brother Richard Hart and Richard's sons Bill, Sherman, and Harry. Capone's nephews saw their uncle as a gentle, lovable man who gave them spending money and enjoyed wrestling with them. "He was a big man, very friendly and outgoing. He was in a fine mood, very happy. He did not appear to be in poor health; he looked just fine,"[108] a friend of Harry's said.

Although Capone appeared fine at times, he was often delusional and disoriented. The FBI, who kept a watchful eye on him because Ralph Capone remained in the crime business and many crime figures visited Palm Island, reported, "[He] is believed to still view himself as the underworld king he once was in Chicago, becoming greatly excited and irritated when his every wish is not immediately fulfilled."[109] Eventually, his speech was unintelligible, he walked jerkily, he experienced tremors and epileptic-type seizures, and his concentration and memory were seriously impaired. He retained only a vague recollection of his time in Alcatraz, and surprised his family by expressing constant praise for the care he had received during his incarceration. Jack Guzik, who saw him during

one of his confused periods, stated, "He is as nutty as a cuckoo."[110]

"My Jesus Mercy"

Because any excitement agitated him, Al Capone celebrated his forty-eighth birthday quietly, surrounded by his family. The anniversary was noteworthy because few criminals of his time reached middle age. Most were gunned down by the police or by one of their rivals at an early age.

Capone's life was drawing to an end, however. On January 19, 1947, about 4:00 A.M. he suffered a stroke. He lay close to death for a week. Then, when doctors thought he was improving, he developed pneumonia, and on the evening of January 25, he died. One historian notes:

> The event occurred without benefit of the gallows, the electric chair, or the machine gun. No one had taken Capone for a ride, leaving his body to be found in three inches of freezing ditch water. At home, in bed, surrounded by grieving relatives, Al Capone died the death of a family man.[111]

In contrast to the lavish funerals of other gangsters, Al Capone's service was quiet and private, allowing his relatives and close friends to mourn the man who had been unswervingly loyal and supportive of them throughout his lifetime. "The

Despite his quiet death, Capone's notorious and violent life left him with a legacy second to none in American history.

public has one idea of my husband," Mae Capone said. "I have another. I will treasure my memory and I will always love him."[112]

After the ceremony, Capone's body was laid to rest in the Mt. Olivet Cemetery in Chicago. Because so many curiosity seekers came to visit the grave, however, the body was later secretly moved across town to a family plot at the Mt. Carmel Cemetery. A modest stone bearing his name and the phrase "My Jesus Mercy" marks the spot.

An Unforgettable Character

Newspapers were quick to note Capone's death. Ordinary Americans, however, took little interest in the gangster's passing. He had been out of the limelight so long that he had become little more than a legend. In fact, many people assumed that he had died long before.

Capone's death was barely newsworthy, but as time passed, America did not forget the great gang lord. He had been too infamous, too grandiose, and too unique for that. He had highlighted Chicago's corruption and revealed the shortcomings of Prohibition. At the same time, he had made millions from them both. His larger-than-life personality, characterized by generosity and

violence, had both charmed and alarmed America. His ability to outwit the system had grabbed and held the country's imagination.

Despite the rise and fall of other crime bosses, serial killers, and public enemies, Capone remained—and still remains—one of the most unforgettable characters on America's roster of notorious individuals. His name became a watchword for gangsterism and corruption. He was reviled as a villain—yet he was saved from being a monster by his loyalty and generosity. "The man did what he had to do," says one of his friends, "and he knew how to do it. He did it the right way."[113] Gangster and gentleman, bully and protector, murderer and family man, Capone is best understood as a product of his times, of his immigrant heritage, and of his passions, both good and bad.

Notes

Introduction:
The Lawless Era

1. Quoted in Laurence Bergreen, *Capone: The Man and His Era.* New York: Simon and Schuster, 1994, p. 22.
2. Bergreen, *Capone: The Man and His Era,* p. 24.
3. Quoted in Bergreen, *Capone: The Man and His Era,* p. 211.
4. Quoted in John Kobler, *Capone: The Life and World of Al Capone.* New York: G.P. Putnam Sons, 1971, p. 221.
5. Frederick Lewis Allen, *Only Yesterday.* 1931. Reprint, New York: Harper Row, 1964, p. 92.
6. Quoted in Bergreen, *Capone: The Man and His Era,* p. 211.

Chapter One:
Hefty Hooligan

7. Quoted in Rick Hornung, *Al Capone.* New York: Park Lane Press, 1998, p. 5.
8. Quoted in Bergreen, *Capone: The Man and His Era,* p. 35.
9. Quoted in Kobler, *Capone: The Life and World of Al Capone,* p. 26.
10. Bergreen, *Capone: The Man and His Era,* p. 49.

11. Quoted in Hornung, *Al Capone,* p. 17.
12. Quoted in Bergreen, *Capone: The Man and His Era,* p. 49.
13. Bergreen, *Capone: The Man and His Era,* p. 50.
14. Quoted in Bergreen, *Capone: The Man and His Era,* p. 51.
15. Quoted in Bergreen, *Capone: The Man and His Era,* p. 57.
16. Quoted in Bergreen, *Capone: The Man and His Era,* p. 58.
17. Quoted in Bergreen, *Capone: The Man and His Era,* p. 37.

Chapter Two:
Turf Wars

18. Quoted in Robert J. Schoenberg, *Mr. Capone: The Real—And Complete—Story of Al Capone.* New York: William Morrow, 1992, p. 62.
19. Quoted in Schoenberg, *Mr. Capone: The Real—And Complete—Story of Al Capone,* p. 23.
20. Quoted in Schoenberg, *Mr. Capone: The Real—And Complete—Story of Al Capone,* p. 41.
21. Quoted in Schoenberg, *Mr. Capone: The Real—And Complete—Story of Al Capone,* p. 64.

22. Quoted in Kobler, *Capone: The Life and World of Al Capone*, p. 67.

23. Quoted in Schoenberg, *Mr. Capone: The Real—And Complete—Story of Al Capone*, p. 68.

24. Quoted in Kobler, *Capone: The Life and World of Al Capone*, p. 102.

25. Quoted in Hornung, *Al Capone*, p. 43.

26. Quoted in Kobler, *Capone: The Life and World of Al Capone*, p. 108.

27. Quoted in "Frank Capone," *Seize the Night*, 2001. www.carpenoctem.tv.

28. Quoted in Hornung, *Al Capone*, p. 52.

29. Quoted in Bergreen, *Capone: The Man and His Era*, p. 115.

30. Kobler, *Capone: The Life and World of Al Capone*, p. 114.

31. Quoted in Bergreen, *Capone: The Man and His Era*, p. 110.

32. Quoted in Bergreen, *Capone: The Man and His Era*, p. 104.

33. Quoted in Bergreen, *Capone: The Man and His Era*, p. 123.

34. Quoted in Marilyn Bardsley, "Al Capone," *The Crime Library*, 2001. www.crimelibrary.com.

35. Bergreen, *Capone: The Man and His Era*, p. 139.

36. Quoted in Kobler, *Capone: The Life and World of Al Capone*, p. 137.

Chapter Three: "There Goes Al!"

37. Quoted in Bergreen, *Capone: The Man and His Era*, p. 149.

38. Bergreen, *Capone: The Man and His Era*, p. 148.

39. Quoted in Schoenberg, *Mr. Capone: The Real—And Complete—Story of Al Capone*, p. 177.

40. Quoted in Hornung, *Al Capone*, p. 113.

41. Quoted in Schoenberg, *Mr. Capone: The Real—And Complete—Story of Al Capone*, p. 180.

42. Quoted in Schoenberg, *Mr. Capone: The Real—And Complete—Story of Al Capone*, p. 181.

43. Kobler, *Capone: The Life and World of Al Capone*, p. 164.

44. Quoted in Bardsley, "Al Capone." www.crimelibrary.com.

45. Quoted in Kobler, *Capone: The Life and World of Al Capone*, p. 175.

46. Quoted in Bergreen, *Capone: The Man and His Era*, p. 171.

47. Quoted in Bergreen, *Capone: The Man and His Era*, p. 184.

48. Quoted in Bergreen, *Capone: The Man and His Era*. p. 192.

49. Quoted in Bergreen, *Capone: The Man and His Era*, p. 214.

50. Quoted in Kobler, *Capone: The Life and World of Al Capone*, p. 195.

51. Quoted in Marilyn Bardsley,

"Eliot Ness: The Man Behind the Myth," *The Crime Library,* 2001. www.crimelibrary.com.

52. Quoted in Bergreen, *Capone: The Man and His Era,* p. 315.

53. Quoted in Schoenberg, *Mr. Capone: The Real—And Complete—Story of Al Capone,* p. 234.

54. Quoted in Schoenberg, *Mr. Capone: The Real—And Complete—Story of Al Capone,* p. 292.

55. Quoted in Bergreen, *Capone: The Man and His Era,* p. 16.

Chapter Four: Family Man

56. Quoted in Bergreen, *Capone: The Man and His Era,* p. 340.

57. Bergreen, *Capone: The Man and His Era,* p. 56.

58. Quoted in Bergreen, *Capone: The Man and His Era,* p. 149.

59. Bergreen, *Capone: The Man and His Era,* p. 283.

60. Bergreen, *Capone: The Man and His Era,* p. 593.

61. Quoted in Kobler, *Capone: The Life and World of Al Capone,* p. 209.

62. Quoted in Schoenberg, *Mr. Capone: The Real—And Complete—Story of Al Capone,* pp. 292–93.

63. Quoted in Bergreen, *Capone: The Man and His Era,* p. 189.

64. Quoted in Schoenberg, *Mr. Capone: The Real—And Complete—Story of Al Capone,* p. 179.

65. Quoted in Schoenberg, *Mr. Capone: The Real—And Complete—Story of Al Capone,* p. 219.

66. Quoted in Schoenberg, *Mr. Capone: The Real—And Complete—Story of Al Capone,* p. 179.

67. Quoted in Bergreen, *Capone: The Man and His Era,* p. 183.

68. Quoted in Bergreen, *Capone: The Man and His Era,* p. 257.

69. Quoted in Schoenberg, *Mr. Capone: The Real—And Complete—Story of Al Capone,* p. 179.

70. Quoted in Bergreen, *Capone: The Man and His Era,* p. 186.

71. Quoted in Bergreen, *Capone: The Man and His Era,* p. 149.

72. Quoted in Bergreen, *Capone: The Man and His Era,* p. 369.

73. Quoted in Bergreen, *Capone: The Man and His Era,* p. 441.

Chapter Five: "Get Capone"

74. Quoted in Bergreen, *Capone: The Man and His Era,* p. 265.

75. Quoted in Bergreen, *Capone: The Man and His Era,* p. 386.

76. Quoted in Bergreen, *Capone: The Man and His Era,* p. 366.

77. Quoted in Kobler, *Capone: The Life and World of Al Capone,* p. 267.

78. Quoted in Schoenberg, *Mr. Capone:*

The Real—And Complete—Story of Al Capone, p. 241.

79. Quoted in Bardsley, "Eliot Ness: The Man Behind the Myth." www.crimelibrary.com.

80. Quoted in Bardsley, "Eliot Ness: The Man Behind the Myth." www.crimelibrary.com.

81. Eliot Ness, *The Untouchables: The Real Story.* New York: Simon and Schuster, 1957, p. 198.

82. Frank J. Wilson, "Undercover Man: He Trapped Capone," *Colliers Magazine*, April 16, 1947, pp. 14–15.

83. Wilson, "Undercover Man: He Trapped Capone," *Colliers Magazine*, p. 14.

84. Wilson, "Undercover Man: He Trapped Capone," *Colliers Magazine*, p. 15.

85. Quoted in Bergreen, *Capone: The Man and His Era*, p. 394.

86. Quoted in Bergreen, *Capone: The Man and His Era*, p. 275.

87. Quoted in Schoenberg, *Mr. Capone: The Real—And Complete—Story of Al Capone*, p. 315.

88. Quoted in Kobler, *Capone: The Life and World of Al Capone*, p. 332.

89. Wilson, "Undercover Man: He Trapped Capone," *Colliers Magazine*, p. 83.

90. Quoted in Bardsley, "Al Capone." www.crimelibrary.com.

91. Quoted in Hornung, *Al Capone*, p. 161.

92. Quoted in Schoenberg, *Mr. Capone: The Real—And Complete—Story of Al Capone*, p. 326.

93. Quoted in Kobler, *Capone: The Life and World of Al Capone*, p. 347.

94. Quoted in Kobler, *Capone: The Life and World of Al Capone*, p. 347.

Chapter Six: Prisoner Number 85

95. Quoted in Bergreen, *Capone: The Man and His Era*, p. 514.

96. Bergreen, *Capone: The Man and His Era*, p. 543.

97. Quoted in Schoenberg, *Mr. Capone: The Real—And Complete—Story of Al Capone*, p. 334.

98. Quoted in Bergreen, *Capone: The Man and His Era*, p. 538.

99. Quoted in Bergreen, *Capone: The Man and His Era*, p. 522.

100. Quoted in Bergreen, *Capone: The Man and His Era*, p. 537.

101. Quoted in Kobler, *Capone: The Life and World of Al Capone*, p. 367.

102. Quoted in Bergreen, *Capone: The Man and His Era*, p. 551.

103. Quoted in Schoenberg, *Mr. Capone: The Real—And Complete—Story of Al Capone*, p. 341.

104. Quoted in Bergreen, *Capone: The Man and His Era*, p. 562.

Chapter Seven:
The Legacy of Capone

105. Bergreen, *Capone: The Man and His Era*, p. 582.

106. Quoted in Bergreen, *Capone: The Man and His Era*, p. 579.

107. Quoted in Kobler, *Capone: The Life and World of Al Capone*, p. 375.

108. Quoted in Bergreen, *Capone: The Man and His Era*, p. 593.

109. Quoted in Bergreen, *Capone: The Man and His Era*, p. 587.

110. Quoted in Schoenberg, *Mr. Capone: The Real—And Complete—Story of Al Capone*, p. 353.

111. Bergreen, *Capone: The Man and His Era*, p. 607.

112. Quoted in Kobler, *Capone: The Life and World of Al Capone*, p. 269.

113. Quoted in Bergreen, *Capone: The Man and His Era*, p. 604.

For Further Reading

Linda Jacobs Altman, *The Decade that Roared: America During Prohibition.* New York: Henry Holt, 1997. A very good account of the 1920s with an emphasis on Prohibition.

Martin Hintz, *Farewell, John Barleycorn: Prohibition in the United States.* Minneapolis: Lerner Publications, 1996. Prohibition and its consequences in the United States.

David C. King, *Capone and the Roaring Twenties,* Woodbridge, CT: Blackbirch Press, 1999. Overview of Al Capone's life and events that marked the 1920s including heroes of the age, the Scopes trial, revival of the Ku Klux Klan, and others.

Alan MacDonald, *Al Capone and His Gang.* New York: Scholastic, 1999. An entertaining look at the life and times of Al Capone.

Karen L. Trespacz, *The Trial of Gangster Al Capone: A Headline Court Case.* Berkeley Heights, NJ: Enslow Publishers, 2001. The book focuses on the government's 1931 prosecution of Al Capone for tax evasion.

Major Works Consulted

Books

Frederick Lewis Allen, *Only Yesterday.* 1931. Reprint, New York: Harper Row, 1964. One of the first histories written about the 1920s, drawn from documents, articles, and statistics of the era. Includes a section on Al Capone.

Laurence Bergreen, *Capone: The Man and His Era.* New York: Simon & Schuster, 1994. A well-written, entertaining work focusing on Al Capone and America of the early 1900s.

Rick Hornung, *Al Capone.* New York: Park Lane Press, 1998. A brief, well-written work. Worth reading to get an accurate overview of Capone's life.

John Kobler, *Capone: The Life and World of Al Capone.* New York: G.P. Putnam Sons, 1971. Fact-filled account of Al Capone's life. Includes several pages of period photos of Capone's early home, his family, rivals, allies, and others.

Eliot Ness, *The Untouchables: The Real Story.* New York: Simon & Schuster, 1957. A highly colored version of Ness's efforts as a Prohibition agent to shut down Al Capone's bootlegging empire.

Geoffrey Perrett, *America in the Twenties: A History.* New York: Simon & Schuster, 1982. An in-depth look at the problems, pursuits, and personalities of the 1920s including Prohibition, crime, and Al Capone.

Robert J. Schoenberg, *Mr. Capone: The Real—And Complete—Story of Al Capone.* New York: William Morrow, 1992. A complete account of Capone's life that includes much never-before-published material. Includes period photos.

Christopher Silvester, ed., *The Norton Book of Interviews.* New York: W. W. Norton, 1993. An anthology of interviews with some of history's most prominent people including Al Capone. Reveals Capone's views on freedom, capitalism, Prohibition, and corruption in America.

Periodicals

Frank J. Wilson, "Undercover Man: He Trapped Capone," *Colliers Magazine,* April 16, 1947. A first-person article relating the activities and adventures of IRS agent Frank Wilson as he attempted to prove tax evasion charges against Al Capone.

Internet Sources

The History Channel, "Five Points Gang," 2001. www.historychannel. com. Short history of the notorious Five Points gang.

Seize the Night, "Frank Capone," 2001. www.carpenoctem.tv. Brief biography of Frank Capone, whose early death cut short what promised to be a brutal crime career.

Websites

The Crime Library (www.crimelibrary. com). The website is dedicated to classic crime stories, gangsters and outlaws, serial killers, spies and terrorists, and crime fiction. Includes an excellent, lengthy segment on Al Capone.

INDEX

PICTURE CREDITS

ABOUT THE AUTHOR

Diane Yancey works as a freelance writer in the Pacific Northwest, where she has lived for over twenty years. She writes nonfiction for middle-grade and high school readers and enjoys traveling and collecting old books. Some of her other books include *Life in the Elizabethan Theater*, *Life in Charles Dickens's England*, *Life in a Japanese American Internment Camp*, and *Life on the Pony Express*.